THE Greatest Survival Stories OF All Time

THE *Greatest Survival Stories OF All Time*

True Tales of People Cheating Death
When Trapped in a Cave, Adrift at
Sea, Lost in the Forest, Stranded
on a Mountaintop, and More

CARA TABACHNICK

Published by:
Ulysses Press
P.O. Box 3440
Berkeley, CA 94703
www.ulyssespress.com

ISBN: 978-1-61243-908-2
Library of Congress Catalog Number: 2018967979

Printed in the United States
10 9 8 7 6 5 4 3 2

Acquisitions editor: Bridget Thoreson
Managing editor: Claire Chun
Editor: Renee Rutledge
Proofreaders: Lauren Harrison, Barbara Schultz
Front cover design: David Hastings
Cover photo: © Davide Foti/Unsplash

Contents

Introduction

Humans believe we have the ability to surmount great adversity. At least, that's what many people, including me, tell ourselves about how we would react when faced with a traumatic situation that we have no control over. But do we? How would we respond if we were caught in an earthquake or a plane crash, or even something more common, such as getting lost on a hike in the desert? All the markers of life that we hold familiar disappear in an instant—and we are left in the maelstrom of uncertainty. In that split second, do we have what it takes to survive?

As I researched and wrote about the following global survival stories, I was overcome by the main characters' abilities not only to make difficult decisions—sometimes in the face of extreme terror—but also to thrive in the aftermath. What was it about these survivors that set them apart? Did an exceptional force live within them? Did they always have the ability to achieve superhuman feats? Or were they just ordinary people blessed with extraordinary grit?

In my quest to discover what set these humans apart, I accessed troves of historical documents, including recently de-classified

spy records from the United Kingdom's National Archives, a ship captain's personal diary retrieved from the Library of Congress, historical newspaper and magazine articles, and a myriad of audio and television interviews to reconstruct these extraordinary stories.

As I reported their experiences, I was struck over and over again by just the simple will to survive. In today's world, we live very orderly lives governed by regulation. Everything, including our food, homes, workplaces, and schools are connected by technology in a way that was unimaginable just a few years ago. In an instant we can get or watch what we want, which has cocooned society in a heterogeneous bubble. There is nothing *primal* about how we exist in today's day and age.

When we read tales of survival, the stories tap into what it means to be connected to our elemental selves. Every person profiled in this book was no more or less than an ordinary human being. What set them apart was their will—and the confidence within themselves to use it. For that is what these survivors have, whether they fell out of a plane, or were lost in the Sahara, or caught spying during the war—they used interior determination to escape the situation. In the end, we are all capable of extraordinary actions. It can just be a matter of how much we believe in ourselves.

This realization was amplified by the audio recordings I listened to during the course of reporting these stories. One was an interview with Juliane Koepcke, the sole survivor of an airplane crash that descended smack in the middle of the Peruvian rain forest. Just a teenager, Juliane was traveling on Christmas Eve with her mother, who died soon after the plane plummeted to the ground. After searching for, but not finding her mother, Juliane managed

to survive for almost eleven days days in the jungle before she was rescued by two woodcutters. She subsisted mostly on water, foraged leaves, and one bag of holiday candy.

As an adult woman recounting her experience, Juliane remembered how after the crash, she felt an instinctive need to survive. She knew she needed to move forward, and even her fear, and the unknown outcome of her mother's life, didn't stop the march. And she wasn't going to, couldn't, give up. Listening to her story made me realize life's fragility and the grip humans place on it when we can feel it slipping away. The ability to thrive in the face of great danger blooms inside all of us.

My hope is that the triumphs of the survivors profiled here help readers understand the value of life when faced with its demise and, for a moment, feel the *pure joy* of living.

Juliane Koepcke
Primal Survivor
Peruvian Rain Forest, 1971

A blinding white light burst off the airplane's fixed wing. The passengers on the flight screamed in horror. Pressure in the main cabin dropped, the tightly packed overhead bins snapped open, and suitcases, books, and presents wrapped in brightly colored Christmas paper fell into the aisles.

The last thing then-17-year-old Juliane Koepcke heard her beloved mother Maria say was, "This is it."

This was not what Juliane had imagined when they arrived at the airport earlier that day on December 24, 1971, for the regularly scheduled flight from Lima to Pucallpa, a rural area in the center of Peru. They had planned to spend December through February, Peru's summer season, with Juliane's father, Hans-Wilhelm, at their biology station in the middle of the rain forest. Noted German ornithologists, Maria and Hans-Wilhelm were experts on Peruvian birds and had spent their whole careers categorizing and studying them. Under their tutelage, Juliane grew up living between Lima, the capital city, and their research stations. She knew both worlds well and loved the benefits of moving between the two. After a demanding school year, she was ready to explore and relax in the fields and jungles where she had spent a large portion of her childhood.

Instead, their plane's takeoff had been delayed seven hours. The airport had been chaotic. Several flights had been canceled the day before and the airlines were mobbed with people trying to get out before Christmas. People pushed and shoved each other as they demanded answers from airport representatives. A general sense of desperation coupled with anger pulsed through the crowd. Everyone was eager to spend time with their families. Even though delayed flights were normal in Peru, Juliane felt frustrated. The night before, she had stayed up late to attend her high school graduation dance, and the day before that had been her graduation itself. It had been a whirlwind of events and endless celebrations. She had been tired, but she hadn't wanted to complain to her mother, as it was because Juliane begged to stay longer in Lima to attend her special events they'd decided to fly on Christmas Eve. "All right," Maria had acquiesced. "We'll fly on the 24th."

The future was bright and exciting for the petite teenage girl teetering on the cusp of adulthood. It was to be her final schoolgirl summer holiday; afterward, Juliane planned to leave the jungle and mountain landscapes of Peru behind for university study in Bonn, Germany. She had dressed for the brief flight in her best: a brightly patterned mini-dress that barely covered her knees and showed off her thin, pale legs. Short skirts had become all the rage for 1970s high school students, and Juliane wore the style well. The colors complemented her ashy blond hair, which curled gently around her delicate features.

Finally, their delayed flight was given clearance for departure. Thirty minutes after national Peruvian airline LANSA Flight 508 had taken off, passengers were offered a small snack and a drink. It was a compact plane, a four-engine Lockheed Electra turboprop that ferried passengers from the capital to the remote plains of central Peru. Juliane and Maria were sitting toward the back of the plane in a three-seater bench. Juliane chose the window seat, her mother was in the middle, and a heavyset man sat by the aisle. The man promptly fell asleep, and Juliane felt a moment of sympathy for her mother, who she knew must be annoyed by the man's girth spilling over her armrest.

Juliane munched on her food, daydreamed, and stared out the window when the plane entered what looked like very thick, heavy storm clouds. Juliane wasn't nervous. She loved to fly and even enjoyed the turbulence. Like everything else in her unique young life, she counted this as an experience. What was there to worry about? Her mother, however, didn't like to fly and said often that she didn't think it was natural for people to fly in a bird made of metal. Still, Maria traveled often for work, rarely displaying any distress.

Juliane wanted to reach over and pat her mother's hand but started to worry when her mother, normally the picture of composure, gripped the armrest so tightly her knuckles were white.

What is happening? Juliane thought. She couldn't ask her mother, as she didn't want to make the situation worse. She sat as her mother did, attempting to appear unruffled and in control, like a grown-up.

Wings Down

The plane began to churn as it entered the dense air in front of the clouds.

People started complaining that they should turn back rather than risk going through the thick storm clouds. Other voices rose in protest; they were only fifteen minutes from their destination and a majority of the passengers wanted to get home for Christmas. The pilots pressed forward. The plane started to buck as it entered heavier turbulence and the clouds grew darker. Lightening flashed around the plane, illuminating her mother's tense face, which made Juliane very, very nervous. Finally, she reached out and gripped her mother's hand.

They couldn't speak. Around them the sounds of crying and weeping filled the air. Juliane bit her lip. She too wanted to cry. None of the other travelers said anything, but every few seconds there was a scream as the plane rocked and brightly decorated Christmas packages and boxed cakes fell from the overhead compartments onto the shoulders and heads of the frightened passengers. Juliane smiled at the sight of the sweets hurling through the air. She thought everyone was going to be very angry their candy and presents were going to be ruined, but then the plane nose-dived into a tight spiral and sped toward the jungle below. Juliane's stomach dropped as the weight of the plane shifted downward. It was moving so fast. There was no time to do anything.

The passengers started to scream desperately as if to stop the mad descent to the earth. In a flash, it was pitch black around them, and all Juliane could hear was the terrible sounds of their screaming. The deep roaring of the engines filled Juliane's head completely, but then in the next moment, all the horrible noise stopped.

There were a few seconds of silence before the body of the plane broke apart two miles above the ground. Metal flew in every direction, raining its burning fuselage onto the ground below. All the passengers were ejected.

Juliane was suddenly outside the plane. She opened her eyes. She was still strapped to the plane's seat bench with the seatbelt across her shoulder. Her head was draped in between her legs. The two seats next to her were empty. Her mother was gone. All she could hear was the whistling of the wind in her ears.

She saw the green, dense canopy of the jungle spinning beneath her legs.

"Where am I?" she thought.

It was an unreal perspective to be dangling above the trees. The golden light of the sun spread through the leafy tops. She raised her head, then the airplane bench slipped, falling through the foliage she had just been admiring. Before Juliane had a chance to fear what was really happening, she passed out.

Surviving the Jungle

When Juliane woke up, a day had passed. Without thinking, she shifted her body and pain shot everywhere. Yet nothing seemed to be broken. Her hands moved, her legs moved. There were deep cuts on her legs and gouges on the backs of her arms, where she thought metal from the plane had scratched her, but she wasn't bleeding too severely. Some of the blood had dried. Her shoulder ached horribly and she couldn't move it very well, but she was cognizant.

"I've survived an airplane crash," she thought.

Although Juliane had severe pain in her head and was in shock, she knew what had happened. After that moment of incredulity, she immediately knew she needed to make her way out of the jungle.

Juliane propelled herself up from the seat (her seatbelt had unbuckled at some point), and stood up perhaps too quickly. The movement made her dizzy and she dropped to her knees, the jungle spinning around her. Maybe she couldn't walk, she thought, and despair filled her mind. She started to shout for her mother. Where was she? Why wasn't she in the seat beside her? What had happened to her? It suddenly registered that her mother and the man who had sat beside her were missing. The reality of the loss hit her hard. Was her mother still alive? Dropping to her knees, Juliane started to crawl around in circles. She screamed "Mama" in Spanish, German, and then English, calling over and over again, but only the telltale sounds of the jungle answered. A screech of a bird, the howl of a monkey, the swish of the leaves. The were no human voices at all.

Juliane willed herself to say calm. Maybe she could find another passenger who had been on the plane. There had to be someone. She kept moving around in tiny circles until the dizziness subsided from her head. Then, slowly, she stood. There was still intense pain in her knee, but she tested herself, placing one foot in front of another. Her weight held. She could walk.

To remain alive Juliane knew she had to make it out of the rain forest. Before the crash, she spent a year and half living with her parents at the Panguana Ecological Research Station, the bird center they founded. The family had taken many trips in the jungle, and during that time she had learned various ways to live in the wilderness. From her time in the rain forest she had become familiar with the intricacies of its perceived darkness and understood how to live among its dangers. She knew that in order to survive, she had to be aware of where she was stepping and the direction in which she was traveling. She marked the tree where she had landed with a distinctive pattern of leaves. Getting disoriented and lost among the trees was a real danger. Everything looked alike on the floor of the jungle. Juliane needed to remember where she had been and not wander around in disoriented circles.

But she couldn't leave the crash site without trying to find anyone else who might be alive. And, most importantly, Juliane didn't want to leave her mother behind. In her mind, her mother had survived the crash, just as Juliane had, and she was probably somewhere close by. She didn't want to believe her mother was dead. Juliane wandered in the crash's immediate area, looking under crumpled leaves and dense foliage, but found nothing but a thin plastic bag of viscous sweets the passengers had brought on board to celebrate the holidays. She didn't even know what day it was. Maybe it was Christmas. She checked her watch and saw the date. She had been right. Less than twenty-fours had passed since the plane had crashed.

Juliane picked up the bag of candies; for now they were the only food she had. She placed one in her mouth, the sweet stickiness offering a brief respite from the trauma she had just experienced. Above her she could hear the muted noise of plane engines roaring. She was sure the government had been alerted and was already searching for crash victims. Juliane couldn't see the planes and there was no possibility for the rescuers to find her because the foliage was so dense. She needed to get to a wide-open space within the jungle, either by a riverbank or jungle town. During her reconnaissance she didn't find any metal fragments; it was as the whole plane had just burst in the air and vanished into pieces.

Juliane's dress was ripped, but maybe the pilots would be able to pick out its bright colors through the trees. She had one white sandal on her left foot; the other had fallen off. As Juliane walked, she stepped forward with the sandaled foot, hoping the flimsy leather would protect her from whatever could jump out from the rain forest. There could be snakes, which camouflaged themselves under the dry leaves that covered the floor of the jungle. During the crash, she had lost her glasses; she was very nearsighted and couldn't see that clearly in front of her, so every step was a risk. She heard a tiny sound like that of water burbling. She followed the noise and found a small spring bubbling from the ground.

Juliane knelt down, cupped her hands, and sipped the fresh water. She had a source from which to drink. She had been very worried about thirst and hunger. There were ways to find food in the jungle, but because it was summer most sources had dried up or, like fruit, weren't in season. Juliane had nothing to use to cut into the numerous palms to suck out their juice. At first, she tried to break some of the leaves she recognized with her hands, because she was scared to touch anything she wasn't familiar with as she knew that many things in the jungle are poisonous. But the stems were too tough and didn't respond to her miniscule pressure. They were cutting her knuckles, forming small rivers of blood across her hands.

But here, in front of her, was water. She popped another candy into her mouth and drank as much of the sweet liquid as she could. Juliane knew because there was a spring there would also be a larger body of water, like a river or pond nearby, and then there was sure to be life. She straightened up, and as best as she could, she followed the sound of the spring, deeper into the jungle with only her intuition to guide her.

Follow the River

On her fourth day of wandering, Juliane found a small creek. Her watch, a gift from her beloved grandmother, had stopped ticking, the face's glass now cloudy and muddy. Before the watch stopped, it had been a comforting link to civilization. She used it to keep time to understand how long she had been lost in the jungle. After it stopped, Juliane still kept the watch strapped on her wrist for comfort. It was very disorienting not to understand what day it was.

Juliane knelt to drink from the creek. She thought filling her body with liquids would be the way to stave off starvation, as she had consumed the bag of candies quickly and was suffering from hunger. Mosquitoes and flies endlessly buzzed around her, biting her legs, arms, and back. Large welts had popped up across her entire body. Her wounds were starting to drip yellow pus and weren't healing. The moist air and constant rain weren't helping the cuts close. She tried to find some aloe leaves to apply a salve to her aching arms, but felt too overwhelmed to forage. She tried not to think too much about her injuries.

Juliane was kneeling in the creek when she heard the sound of a king vulture. It landed with a loud thump, a noise she had heard often while living in the research station with her parents. She understood the significance of a vulture; there must be a number of carcasses nearby. They would only land for raw, bloody meat. Dread filled her mind. She felt the corpses of her fellow passengers from the doomed flight must be nearby. She didn't want to be a witness to what that could mean, so she hurried away from the spot.

As Juliane walked around a curve, she saw a three-seat plane bench rammed head down into the creek wall, the flowing water trickling around the heavy obstruction. Buckled into the seats were three passengers. The top half of their bodies, including their heads and shoulders, were inside the earth, covered in mud. All she could see of them were their legs and lower torsos hanging over the side of the seat. They were surely dead. To Juliane it looked like they had been killed upon the impact of the crash.

Looking at the bodies, she felt a sense of relief, knowing they likely hadn't suffered. It was the first time Juliane had seen a corpse. Panic washed over her. She didn't know what to do and felt an urge to run from the scene. Then she thought about her mother. Maybe one of the dead bodies was her mother? Juliane knew this wasn't possible—her mother had been sitting in the three-seater next to her, and when she had woken after the crash the other seats were empty.

Even so, Juliane felt compelled to check. She approached the bench. She touched the corpulent, bloated feet of the corpses with a stick gathered from the riverbed. They had been in the water for quite a few days by now. As she got closer, she could see their flesh had been nibbled at by all sorts of animals, evidenced by bloody gaping holes. She was too scared to touch them with her bare hands.

With the end of the twig, she poked their toes. They didn't move. Juliane bent forward to examine the toes of the dead woman and saw that her toenails were brightly painted. Immediately she knew it couldn't be her mother, as Maria had never painted her feet with polish. Relief flooded Juliane's body, then she felt immense guilt that she was happy at another person's demise. The possibility that she could find her mother still alive filled her mind.

Hope rose again and elated, Juliane set back off into the rain forest, as she made her way through the flooded banks. She was tired and starving. As she rested, huddled under a tree, she saw not one other person. At night, cold rain poured down upon her, leaving her soaked in the morning, her mini dress, which had been shredded into tatters, a poor protection against the ravages of the jungle.

Days later, her strength rapidly fading, Juliane stumbled upon the wide, broad mouth of a river. She felt a moment of salvation. Maybe she would be rescued after all. Juliane knew if there was a river, certainly there was going to be a village close to its shores. Following the bends of the riverbanks proved to be a herculean task. Its shorelines were too dense, overgrown with vines and weeds, and it was a frustrating exercise trying to find a clear path. Juliane knew that stingrays rested on the riverbanks, so she treaded carefully, understanding that if she came upon one, the animal could spear or poison her in fear.

She had been wandering in the jungle for many days and had reached a new level of despair. She heard sounds of chickens and dogs, and was worried she was delirious. She could barely walk; all her energy had diminished. After five days without eating, hunger had long since dulled. Her head throbbed and she couldn't think clearly or figure out which direction to go. She began to fear that no one would ever find her. It had been days since she heard the sounds of planes overhead. She would likely die alone in the rain forest.

Juliane decided to build a raft to drift in the water in the hope that the currents would bring her downstream to some sort of civilization. She gathered some fallen wooden logs and lashed them together with strong vines she found lying on the ground. She tied the knots and surveyed her work. It was a rudimentary but sturdy raft, and she felt proud that she had been able to construct such a contraption in her state. She lowered the raft into the gentle currents, then carefully lowered herself onto the logs and lied down, her blond hair fanning out behind her as she twirled her fingers in the water. The raft drifted downstream, following the river's currents. Part of her wanted to give up and let the warm water wash over her, bringing her along its depths.

At night Juliane lifted herself out of the river, dragging the raft behind her and finding a place on the banks where she could sleep. The unstable contraption soon broke apart, so Juliane decided to swim. She knew she could only swim in the center of the river so as to avoid the piranhas and stingrays that populated the waters. One bite from those dangerous predators and she would perish. With each sodden stroke, Juliane took a leap of faith. Every time she turned her head, she swallowed a mouthful of muddy river water, so her lungs felt waterlogged and heavy.

Every day she swam for hours, the pain between her shoulder blades intense. At night she dozed for a few hours under the cover of bushes, the cacophony of the jungle singing its forlorn songs.

Reaching Civilization

On the tenth day alone in the jungle, toward the late afternoon, Juliane was looking for a slope or a big tree root where she could shelter and rest for the night when she saw a very large boat. She rubbed her eyes with her fists three times. Each time she opened them, the boat was still there, she wasn't hallucinating. It had to be real. Adrenaline raced through her body. Juliane approached the hull of the boat and touched its solid wood, feeling its gritty, splintered side. On the side of the boat was a small dirt path trampled into the jungle. There had to be human habitation nearby.

Juliane set off along the trail, picking her way through the long grass. It was a slow, treacherous climb, as she was very weak from lack of food and water. It took her more than half an hour to ascend a few feet, but still, she persevered, grasping onto roots and branches while making her way up the climb.

Days of brilliant sunshine had blistered her fair skin, leaving red burns across her shoulders and arms. Maggots had infested the deep cuts she received upon the crash's impact. She felt as if she had been scrambling for hours. With a last push of strength, she finally reached the top of the slope.

At the pinnacle, Juliane spotted a hastily constructed hut covered with a braided palm leaf roof. She surmised it was a resting home for jungle woodcutters. Juliane had witnessed the squabbling of traders as they trekked into the jungle looking for the precious woods. They often came into the deep rain forests to cut down trees and send them in boats down river, where timber was harvested and sold in worldwide markets.

In front of the hut sat an outboard motor that Juliane guessed went with the boat, along with a large jug of gasoline. There was no other sign of life. At first, Juliane decided to sit and wait. But after an hour or so when nobody arrived, she opened the top of the gasoline tank. A memory had flashed into Juliane's mind when she saw the gas. During the time her family had lived together at their biological station, their family dog had been sniffing around and cut his leg on a metal scythe. Quickly the deep gash had become infested with maggots, not unlike Juliane's arm, and their beloved animal was in excruciating pain. Her father had flushed out their dog's leg with kerosene, and his infection had healed.

By this time the white and tan squirmy maggots on Juliane's arm had grown over a centimeter. She could feel them moving inside her skin.

With trembling fingers, Juliane tried to open the cap of the gasoline tank. Her fingers were weak and she had problems unscrewing the stopper, which was partially rusted to the tank. It was hard to jostle, but eventually she succeeded. Inside the container was a small tube to siphon the gas. Juliane took the tube into her mouth and sucked the liquid, filling her cheeks. She spat the fuel onto her fingers and then rubbed them into the wound where the maggots were twisting. The liquid entered her cuts and she felt a searing, heavy pain spread throughout her arms. The maggots were desperate to flee the chemicals, and finally, crawled out of her gashes and dropped to the ground. With her fingernails, Juliane pulled out thirty more maggots and felt proud she was able to accomplish her goal. She patted some more gasoline on her wounds to make sure they would heal and wouldn't get infected.

She spent the night sleeping in the empty woodcutter hut. The next day, when Juliane peeled open her eyes, she saw that it was raining heavily and the skies were gray and overcast. She spent most of the day resting under the cover of the palm roof. Since the crash she had not stopped. Every second had been spent on the move. Now, in the relative safety of the hut, she felt the intensity of her struggle catch up. All the pain started. Her body felt as if it were on fire. She felt too weak to get up again. Her plan was to rest for the day, let her cuts heal and her body recover a bit, and start out in the morning. Satisfied, Juliane closed her eyes and dozed off.

By the late afternoon, as Juliane slept on and off, she heard the distinct sound of voices. Because it had been so long since she'd heard another utterance, she thought maybe she was hallucinating. She poked her head out of the doorway to find there were several men speaking outside. To Juliane, it was like hearing the voices of angels. She hadn't heard another human in almost eleven days, and she had been starting to think she never would again.

At first, the men didn't know she was there. When she walked outside, they all turned around and almost jumped out of their skin at Juliane's approach. Seeing a white, fair-skinned, blond-haired girl come suddenly out of their hut, the men thought Juliane was an apparition or a water goddess. Born and raised in the jungle, some of the workers had never even seen a white girl before.

They were jabbering away, unsure of what to do when Juliane responded to their questions in perfect Spanish. She explained that she was the survivor of a plane crash and she had been in the rain forest. Their fears evaporated, and they immediately asked how they could help. Later that afternoon, two more men, Amado Pereya and Marcio Rivera, joined the group.

They fed her little pieces of food at a time, some bread and flattened pieces of fish, and listened to her tell her story. The next morning Amado and Marcio brought Juliane to the medical outpost at the jungle camp Tournavista, where nurse Amanda de Pina tended to the various woodcutters and missionaries who came through their remote part of the country. Juliane was so disoriented and dehydrated, and could barely recount her ordeal to the nurse. Amanda tended to Juliane, and she recovered quickly once given food and liquids. The nurse decided to move her to the hospital at an American missionary center in Pucallpa, Peru.

There was a faint knock on the hospital room door. Juliane's father, Hans-Wilhelm, arrived to see his daughter. He cracked the door open and walked toward her bed. Juliane sat up; she couldn't believe she was seeing her father's face again. After weeks of dreaming of this reunion, she was speechless. He stared at her, saying more with his eyes than words could have ever expressed. Then he held his daughter in his arms. She was going to live, and he was in awe of her strength.

Finally, her father asked, "How are you doing?"

"I'm fine," Juliane answered.

And, in that moment, she truly was.

Juliane Koepcke was the only survivor of the LANSA plane crash on December 24, 1971, that killed 91 other passengers, including her mother. Her experience has been the subject of numerous books, including her own memoir, *When I Fell from the Sky: The True Story of One Women's Miraculous Survival*, and a documentary film. She currently lives in Germany, works as a biologist and librarian at the Bavarian State Collection of Zoology, and flies back to Peru twice a year to manage biological field stations.

Henri Nemy
Pit of Despair
Courrières Coal Mine, Northern France, 1906

Just before 7 a.m. on March 10, 1906, the Courrières mine was already humming. There was no warning about the death and destruction about to come.

As the main employer in this northern French region, the mine saw two thousand men arrive daily, many from the quaint cobblestoned village of Béthune just 18 miles away. Others came from Lille and Courrières, another small town with a population of about four thousand from which the mine adopted its name. Here, working men were coal miners. That's just what they did. Families were supported by coal; bread was baked, babies were born, and life in these towns was guided by the mines' ringing bells. Miles of lush countryside were interrupted by the desecration of extensive coal fields, as dirt hills dotted pastures and ragtag children skipped among them.

That fateful March day, just weeks away from spring, had been chilly and the skies were overcast; winter's long arm still had its hold. Most workers had arrived by 5:30 a.m., and after they changed into their mining clothes, they lined up to be lowered into one of the subterranean pits that made up the complex. Each station consisted of levels of interconnecting steel tracks, interior pits, and horse stables. Steel-caged elevators hauled down groups of workers into each station.

Nothing alerted them to the inferno awaiting. Boom! In a split second, at the entrance of Courrières Coal Mine, a man was no more. His body split apart into molecules of dust from the intensity of the fiery explosion. There was no trace left. Plumes of intense heat destroyed everything in their path. The desperate whinnying of a horse echoed as the force of the explosion lifted the animal off its hooves, singeing its thick mane. Clouds of methane gas followed, filling the crisp air with the foul odor of rotten eggs.

In an instant the mines were a fireball. Flames broke out along the grassy tops of the surrounding fields, and the noxious gases were overwhelming. Rescuers ran toward the pits, dragging men away who were caught on fire, their hair and fingers burning. They pushed these yowling men to the ground in an effort to stomp out the flames. From their offices, mine directors rang alarm bells, informing all towns in the region of the emergency happening at Courrières. The persistent peals could be heard throughout the fields.

Rumors of destruction started to spread, and families began flooding the mines asking for news of loved ones. Makeshift fences had been immediately constructed during the rescue effort, but concerned families started pushing against the fragile bindings, causing the barriers to buckle and break. Detachments of police and cavalry were called into the area to maintain law and order.

The mine's tunnels and elevators were covered by a series of wooden, shed-like structured roofs; in the center of each, a large red-brick chimney loomed. These chimneys, which spouted smoke generated from the mining work below, could be seen from every house across the county and symbolized the powerful nature of the industry. One of the roofs had been blown off by the force of the explosion, its demolished bricks splayed over the ground.

Nearby, another chimney was teetering, about to fall onto the hard, muddy ground. Openings for the primitive steel elevators were arranged in a semi-circle for pits 2, 3, 4, 8, and 10. But now these shafts had also become a deadly weapon: Gases poured from the entrance of pit no. 2, and rescuers couldn't move into the area to pull out the miners. The gases were impossible to see, but their pungent, deadly smell could kill those who inhaled them. They needed to stay away until the air cleared. Many of the rescuers couldn't bear to see their fellow miners die such horrible deaths. From below, terrible screams could be heard. Soldiers and other volunteers tied handkerchiefs around their faces and plunged into the darkness, descending in the elevators to retrieve the men.

Death Tolls Mount

Four hundred local soldiers arrived to hold back the crowds of mourners trying to break into the mine pits. Distraught relatives threw insults and vegetables at the soldiers. Chaos reigned and quickly escalated as it became clear that rescue attempts were hampered by the lack of trained personnel in France at the time. In pit no. 3, the cages were broken and help couldn't get any farther in. Rescuers knew they had to let the hundreds of men there perish and concentrate on saving those in other shafts who still stood a chance at survival. The day before the accident, a fire was reported deep in the mines, but was not extinguished due to a flurry of coal dust. So the miners understood the damage below was sure to be substantial.

About an hour and a half after the explosion, the first cage pulled up fifteen miners who had inhaled the poisonous gas leaked from the explosion. They had covered their mouths and noses with their shirts and groped their way to the exit just in time, and were still alive. The men were taken immediately to the hospital.

A cheer went up through the central room where the miners entered the pits, but was quickly extinguished by the next load to arrive from pit no. 10. On the floor of the cage were the bodies of two dead men who had been suffocated by the noxious gas, and the fear was that the rest of the workers in that pit had met that same fate. A pall fell over the crowd.

Things went from bad to worse.

"It is indescribable. Everything was demolished or had fallen in. I saw bodies lying in piles. My son is below," one miner who had survived the blast told gathered newspaper reporters.

As the rescuers worked to bring up the men, screams kept coming from the shafts below and their chilling sounds filled the mines.

The cages kept pulling up mutilated bodies piled one on top of the other, all completely naked and with a slimy coating of sweat. Their clothes had been disintegrated by the blast. Some of the miners were decapitated. There were body trunks without limbs and detached hands and feet. There were piles of bleeding flesh; the whole sight was an evil-smelling, loathsome human morass. When touched, the blackened piles fell apart in bundles, like pieces of saturated tinder. The survivors vomited at the sight of their fellow brethren. Some were so decimated there was no way to identify the men. The deceased were stacked up haphazardly on three-wheeled mining carts, with blankets thrown over grimacing faces, broken bodies, and crushed limbs.

About six hundred miners were able to reach the surface in the hours that followed the explosion. But they weren't in the clear; many were severely burned or suffered from the effects of mine gases. As the news spread throughout the region, more families arrived to see if their loved ones had survived. They shouted for news from officials.

M. Lavaurs, the director of the mine, stepped out to address the waiting families.

His face was solemn and drawn.

"Of 1,800 miners who were down in the pits when the explosion occurred," he explained, "in pit no. 4, 673 men were working; 482 men in pit no. 3; in pit no. 2, 571; and the remainder in pit no. 10. At the present moment more than 1,000 men remained imprisoned."

Silence fell upon those gathered as they processed the information. If the numbers were correct, it meant almost all of the day's workers had perished.

Another director standing besides Lavaurs corrected him, saying the men in the mine more likely numbered around 1,100.

"Have you still any hope?" a single voice from the crowd called out.

In a quiet voice Lavaurs responded, "No, I believe all of them are dead."

Trapped Underground

Down below, 38-year-old Henri Nemy had been knocked over by the force of the explosion. Stick-thin, with dark black hair and stooped shoulders, Henri wore a permanently surprised expression on his face. Henri was built for this type of work. A lifelong miner, he had learned the trade from family members; his father and his grandfather worked with coal as he did. Through his elders, Henri had heard tales of mine blasts, and although he had never directly been caught in one, he had enough sense to know how to act.

Knowing that the only way to survive an explosion of this size was not to breathe in the gas, Henri got to his feet, pulling his heavy fabric jacket over his mouth. He could hear screams from above, but where he was in mine shaft no. 2 it was completely dark, as the explosion had knocked out all of the electricity that normally lit the gas lamps lining the tunnels' expanses.

The mine's work tunnels were lined with thick, sawn timber and braced on each side with similar joist-like logs. Their imposing, solid edifice was designed to provide a sense of safety that the walls wouldn't collapse on them, as the men used their pickaxes to carve out the black coal embedded in the earth. Puffs of dust floated in the air as the men plucked out the soft substance. Wooden carts ran back and forth on steel tracks, filled to the brim with coal. Miners strode alongside the tracks, their axes slung over their shoulders, stopping every few feet to forage for coal. Steel elevators lifted the coal out of the belly of the mine to its entrance. Even though he couldn't see an inch in front of him, Henri knew the mine's familiar confines like the back of his hand.

Henri pulled his thick blue cloth jacket over his nose and stumbled through the damaged tunnels, searching for an area where he could breathe air. The key, he knew, was not to panic. If he panicked his lungs would constrict. All of the mine's complex infrastructure now served as a threat to Henri's very survival. Several timbers had cracked and fallen over, blocking passageways and making it incredibly difficult to trace his steps back toward the entrance. The steel tracks had twisted and come off their hinges, leaving sharp edges sticking in the electrical wires that had broken and frayed.

Once the outside entrances were closed off and the fires that normally warmed the mines were put out, Henri knew within hours the pits would be freezing. Blocked off from the other shafts and tunnels, the mine he was walking in was growing colder and darker. A damp chill filled the air. He didn't see any other fellow miners or anyone moving. Surely, he couldn't be the only survivor. He couldn't let himself think about that now. With his already-icy fingers, he felt for the watch that he kept in his inside jacket pocket. He pulled the chain of his timepiece out and wound the dial, ensuring it would keep running for another few hours. It was almost completely dark in the mines and there was no way to keep track of day or night.

If the watch died and Henri lost track of time, he would surely perish. Underground workers depended on knowing which hour it was to keep their own circadian rhythms in check. Without a sense of day or night, workers began to feel anxious. Miners knew the lack of light played tricks on the mind; working in the dark had its own curses: Mistakes were made. Claustrophobia was common. Workers turned on each other. Each miner kept strict observation of the time.

As Henri began moving, feeling his way through the darkness, he knocked into a body with each step he took. They were piled on top of each other. Henri didn't want to stop to consider if they had a pulse. He knew he must try to find a way to exit if he was going to make it out of the mines alive. Steeling his heart, he stepped over countless comrades and walked for what seemed liked hours; in reality, it was only a few minutes before he came to what seemed like a niche in the mine's wall. In the darkness he heard what sounded like the murmur of men's voices. Using his hands to guide him, he made his way along the shaft into the indent to find a group of about twenty miners huddled in the corner.

"Hello," Henri called softly, raising his hands outside his jacket to show he wasn't a threat to them. He wasn't sure how these young miners would respond under such immense pressure. All of them were in their teens and twenties, and there was fear in their eyes. This was the first explosion they had ever seen. Henri saw the 17-year-old son of one of the men who worked in the mine. He was just a boy. Henri knew he had to take command. He assembled the group, now squarely under his charge.

"Whatever happens, we can't sleep more than a few winks at a time," Henri instructed. He tapped his watch; it was still working. "We'll use this to keep track of the time."

"Can we not even close our eyes?" Lefebvre, one of the youngest miners, asked.

"If we sleep, we will die," said Henri firmly.

He knew he had to shut down any sign of rebellion within the men. If the men didn't listen to his rules, Henri didn't think they would be able to safely navigate the mine's difficulties and they would surely perish.

Henri further explained to his compadres that he was worried about the gases seeping into their mouths while they were sleeping. They would inhale the fumes and, without knowing it, suffocate and die. They had to stay awake and be vigilant enough to keep their shirts pressed over their mouths.

Somehow the ragtag group had trudged to pit no. 10, the most remote part of the mine that was rarely used. Coal didn't flow easily there, and only the most hardened or newest miners were sent. The directors convinced junior miners that it was good training to learn how to coax coal from its reluctant mistress. Experienced miners were paid extra to extract it from the difficult tunnels. Henri understood the chances of being discovered here were slim. First, there weren't as many miners in this part of the complex, and second, rescuers wouldn't have been able to make it through the burning ball of fire that engulfed the top floors.

Smoke and the scent of charred bodies wafted through the tunnels, engulfing their noses. Even though the flames hadn't traveled to the lower floors, Henri could only imagine what chaos the fire was causing in the pits above. He knew they had to wait for the fire to burn out before they could move toward the entrance. In order to survive the unknown wait, they needed shelter from the cold, food, and, most importantly, they needed water. Henri formulated some ideas, and as he explained his plan to the boys, the walls of the mine started to move and shake, sending a shower of rocks down from the walls.

The tremor completely blocked the entrance of the niche where the men huddled. The rocks piled on top of each other, entombing the men inside. Within minutes they were completely blocked in. Any hint of light and air coming in through the porous rocks was gone from the small space. Henri could hear one of the younger miners begin to weep. Hope that had been building moments before now evaporated. Chances of escape appeared to be slim.

Above ground, the French government scrambled. As official estimates of deaths started to accumulate, it became clear that the disaster was larger than the administration could have ever imagined. During the first days after the explosion they recovered almost 1,000 corpses. Authorities had to send the army to place the bodies in the coffins. There surely wasn't enough manpower to load body pieces blown apart by the blast of the explosion. Parts were just shoveled into various coffins, and complete corpses were placed in white wooden coffins with a black cross painted on top. It was a grotesque operation.

Three priests stood nearby to encourage soldiers in their backbreaking, sorrowful work. Each priest said a benediction over the deceased miner before the coffin was nailed shut. Around the clock, gravediggers spent hours shoveling mounds of dirt. Freshly dug graves dotted the farmlands.

Survival Tactics

Down in pit no. 10, Henri and the men were desperate to break out of the tomb in which they were trapped. But Henri cautioned the eager miners not to knock down the rocks; the mine structure was unstable and they needed to be careful. One at a time, the rocks had to come down. As they dismantled them, the miners scraped water from the porous stones and saved the liquid drop by drop to drink. As some of the men started the fragile work of dismantling the wall, Henri sent the others to search the small area for possible food. Behind their niche was a small alleyway, the men said, but in the end they found nothing for nourishment, just rocks and the timber holding up the walls.

"We'll have to use this," Henri said and knocked on the wooden structure.

He directed the men to tear strips off the rotting bark, and chew the wood into tiny pieces. Guided by their hunger, the men ripped the dry bark into strips and chewed. They pushed it into the back of their throats so it simulated food and turned into a mushy paste. In that manner, by eating the timber and licking the stones dry, the miners subsisted in that enclosure for eight days. Each day they took down the porous rocks until they finally made a hole big enough to climb through.

Outside the passage was the darkest black any of them had ever experienced, an inky obsidian that made it impossible to see in front of them. The men navigated through the hole in the makeshift wall and headed into the outlying abyss. Henri could feel trepidation in the movements of his followers, but he pressed them to proceed nonetheless. The only way to inch forward was by touch, a combination of putting their hands on the bony shoulders of the men in front of them and alongside the collapsed shafts of the mine.

One wrong move would bring disaster. The men moved cautiously behind their leader. If he stopped and tripped, the line of men toppled. It was slow going, and there were many moments the men had to stop. For days they walked in the dark like this, only stopping to lick moisture from the rocks.

By the fourth day of their trek, Henri couldn't judge if they were any closer to the entrance. He felt a dip in the mine's walls, and Henri knew his group stumbled into one of the stables. Every mine pit had one or two stables where they kept the "pit ponies." From the age of four, these horses lived solely underground, only going above ground once a year for mining celebrations. The rest of their time was spent hauling up to 30 tons of coal daily. The horses worked eight hours a day, and most died within three years of entering the mines. Their lives were hard and desolate, and the miners were indifferent to their plight, as their lives, too, suffered. The horses did the lion's share of the heavy work. Still, the stables below were built well, with timbered ceilings and stalls filled high with hay. Groomers took care of the horses, feeding them carrots and, sometimes, apples.

As they entered the stables, the miners could feel the cold bodies of the dead horses with the tips of their feet. The gases had felled these animals, who now lay dead on the floor of their home, their flesh quickly turning putrid.

"Let's rest here and see what we can find," Henri told his group. The men rummaged around the ground, sifted through the decaying hay, and some shoved handfuls into their mouths, as if they were cows chewing on their cud. At last, a shout came from Leon Boursier, one of the quietest and youngest members of the group. He had been searching the farthest stalls.

"Carrots," Boursier called out, holding up a sickly orange bunch, which had been crumbled underneath the dry hay. They must have been brought down by one of the stable hands the morning of the explosion. Now, the withered bunch of vegetables seemed the greatest delight on earth. The men feasted on the carrots, dividing them carefully among them. Almost two weeks had passed since they'd eaten any real food, and the men savored each bite of the dried vegetable.

"This is our best meal," said Boursier.

Henri knew the food they had to eat next wasn't going to be as satisfying. If they were going to survive the mines, they needed strength and protein to get the blood circulating through their bodies again. They needed to eat meat. There was no doubt they needed to eat the horses.

Many of the miners had steel knives on them to dislodge stubborn rocks or coal during mining. Henri directed them each to a horse. He nodded his head. The men knew what to do. Kneeling beside the sturdy animals, they sawed off pieces of the horses' forelocks, back, or side of the head by the thinning mane and grimly chewing the putrid, raw meat. It took all of their energy not to regurgitate the bloody meat back on the hard mud ground. But they swallowed, firmly lodging the protein into their stomachs.

The cold had become intense in the past few days as the fires above smoldered and burned out. There was no way to light a fire. Huddling together didn't stave off the frigid air or temper the cold. Some of the men's limbs had turned blue, including their feet, and Henri worried his fellow miners would suffer from hypothermia. He had all the men rub their hands and feet together. They slept with their hands interlinked for warmth. Still, it wasn't enough.

Above ground, the mine company directors had called off the search and rescue. It had been more than two weeks since the explosion. Lauer, one of the organization's top engineers, believed that any remaining miners had died long before. He told the bosses there was no way they could have survived the blast, the mines, the cold, or the smoldering fires. Lauer rationalized that anyone left must have starved to death or perished from exhaustion. Many of the mine's tunnels had been sealed off or blocked by falling rocks, with no way to escape.

It was time to send in the local salvage crews. Men gathered from nearby towns to pry away and collect scraps of loose metal, wood, or anything of value that could be sold. The longer the shafts were closed, the more money was being lost. Directors wanted to reopen the mine and begin picking coal again. The living men were out of work, with no money coming into their pockets. They had families to support, and the mining towns were starting to get restless. Dissatisfaction rose among the men, then protests. They were hungry and poor and wanted the mines to reopen. They started to point fingers. Leadership gave in to the demands of the workers, and the work of cleaning up and reopening the mines began.

Some of the pits escaped unscathed from the explosion, and once the gases dissipated, they were usable. Engineers judged them safe to enter. The crews were sent down below day and night, working twenty-four-hour shifts in a frenzied effort. Distraught wives still gathered at the gates of the mine, hoping for word about the missing men. So many never got news about their missing husbands, sons, or brothers. Not everyone pulled out of the pits was identified, so many still held out hope their family members were alive. When they saw that salvage crews were being sent into the pits, indignant cries arose. "We will dig our husbands out," one wife cried. "Give us tools!"

They didn't know that underneath the ground they stood on, men were still alive and fighting to get out.

An Unlikely Escape

Down below, a sliver of sky appeared in the distance, and even the weak glimmer of light was too harsh for the miners' sullied eyes. They had been trapped underground for twenty days, and right in front of them was the freedom they had so desperately sought. It almost couldn't be believed. For the last few hours, they had been following the draft of fresh air smelled by the weakest of the miners, Martin. Henri thought he must have been delusional. For days the men thought they saw various things and called out along their route, but in the end it turned out to be just that, a vision. But then, the fresh air wafted by him and the other men. It had been the first time they had gotten a whiff of the outside since descending into the mine pits so many weeks ago.

During the last hours of their captivity, the miners followed this beguiling current, which was being driven into that part of the mine by a ventilator. They arrived at a barrier formed by a fallen roof. In front of them, Henri could see the elevators, which would carry them above ground. At first, Henri crawled toward the steel cage, rallying the men behind him. "We are almost out," he cried softly, seeing the cages ahead of them and wisps of daylight streaming down the mine shafts.

He had watched their wasted bodies collapse, some from dehydration and some from hunger. Others just fell off as they were groping along in the dark. Henri couldn't stop or retrace their steps to try and find those who had been lost. The survival of the remaining men depended on them moving forward.

Just remnants of Henri's voice remained, but he wanted the surviving men to know they were almost there. His voice was raspy and hoarse from the days of barely drinking and eating. Over the past few days, the men had tried not to talk at all, conserving their strength. Ahead of them was a gang of rough salvagers who had just finished their night's work breaking down the twisted steel and wood destroyed by the blast. The feeble, distraught miners appeared in front of the salvagers. They recoiled in shock.

"We are alive," Henri called to the befuddled men who watched the group suddenly appear. "We are real."

The salvagers bundled the men onto the elevator and rode up with them. As the steel cage shot up toward the sky, no one said a word, so confused they were by the miracle taking place in front of them. The miners stumbled out, dazzled by bright sunlight, which they hadn't seen for almost a month. They were covered in black soot, including their arms and entire faces, from their lips to their eyes. Only the whites of their eyes were showing. Their clothes were ravaged, and their bodies were skin and bones. Some men couldn't speak, and their lips were chapped and blistered.

"We just want to go home," one of the survivors said feebly, looking around for the wives and children he had imagined would be waiting for them. He did not genuinely understand that so many days had passed and that everyone assumed no more men would make it out of the mine alive. Families had stopped standing vigil as the salvagers began their work.

Using their last bit of strength, the men covered their eyes with their arms in a valiant effort to block the harsh sunlight. In the end, thirteen men made it out of the mining disaster—over the past few difficult weeks Henri had lost seven to death. The men started to weep at the sight of the land and their freedom. The hardened scavengers started to cry alongside them in awe of these men who had survived so much.

After it became obvious that they could hardly stand or speak, were malnourished and close to death, the men were rushed to the hospital. Their relatives were informed of their loved ones' survival and they rushed to see them. In haste, Henri's wife arrived, dressed in the stiff black mourning outfit she had been wearing for the past few weeks, to find her husband lying alive in his hospital bed.

He sat up, a grin on his haggard and pale face, and asked, "Why are you wearing mourning?"

The Courrières Coal Mine explosion was the second-worst mining explosion in history, with over 1,000 miners killed in the tragedy. Henri Nemy and twelve other miners survived underground following the disaster for twenty days. They were the largest known group of survivors to emerge from the wreckage. As a result of the explosion, the French coal industry joined other countries in monitoring coal dust.

Enietra Washington
Point-Blank Range
Southside, Los Angeles, 1988

Enietra Washington walked into the packed courtroom. Every row was tightly packed with spectators. She never thought this day would come. Twenty-eight years had passed since she'd survived a fateful night on November 7, 1988. Now it was 2016. She was a different woman. There was no fear in her countenance. Just determination. She threw back her shoulders ready to speak, and nothing would be able to stop her words. Her attacker, Lonnie Franklin, Jr., sat behind wire mesh, separating them. He was wearing an ill-fitting orange jumpsuit with the words "Los Angeles County Jail" printed on the back. Perched on his nose were thick black-framed glasses that complemented his receding salt-and-pepper hairline and perfectly groomed mustache. Deep into middle age, he looked small and harmless.

But Enietra knew differently.

She took a deep breath, and her silver and turquoise hoop earrings that matched so well with her flower-printed, blue tank top jangled.

She wanted to look happy during this essential moment. She felt the wonder of her survival and grief for the women that didn't make it, empowered as she stepped up to take the stand.

"My name is Enietra Washington, and I am one of your victims," she said, nodding once at Lonnie.

"Your only living victim."

On the Prowl

There had been something sweet about the man as he sat expectantly in the orange Ford Pinto with the white racing stripe painted onto the front hood. His thick-rimmed, nerdy glasses and black button-up polo shirt certainly didn't match the gaudiness of his pimped-out car. She'd noticed his shirt was tucked neatly into his khaki pants.

Enietra was intrigued. After all, it was Saturday night in Los Angeles on November 7, 1988, and after a long and emotional breakup with her husband and a visit down South with her relatives in Louisiana, Enietra was looking for a distraction. She was only thirty years old and had a lot of living left to do. Tall and curvy with curly, short brown hair and flashing eyes, Enietra didn't want her ex-husband to bring her down. He was just one man. She wanted to feel good. To feel alive. To feel sexy. She was headed to a party with her long-time best friend, Lydia, who'd promised that a night of dancing with some good-looking guys would cheer her up. Even though it was already November, the night was still warm, so Enietra had decided to walk over to Lydia's house, which was just a ten-minute stroll from hers, when she was stopped by the stranger in the car.

The tricked-out car slid up to the cement curb, its engine idling and tailpipe blowing out smoke. At first, Enietra ignored the driver. She had enough sense to know not to stop and talk to anyone. But the car kept pulling up and following her.

Finally, Enietra stopped.

She peeked further into the Pinto. She was impressed by the cleanliness of its interior and diamond-patterned white leather bucket seats. It went well with her white miniskirt, and the seats were spotless. There wasn't a scrap of dirt or food anywhere, something she didn't often see on the southside of Los Angeles. The stick shift looked like a cue stick with a white pool ball on top. Maybe she'd judged the driver too harshly. Before she could apologize, however, he spoke.

"Come on, I'll give you a ride," said the stranger.

Enietra considered the prospect. He seemed fairly innocuous. It was either accept a ride or walk another ten minutes. Usually, she didn't mind wandering through the streets of her beloved neighborhood. But in the 1980s, her familiar stomping grounds had become dangerous. Gangs had taken over the streets, and there was an ongoing war between the Bloods and the Crips. Crack was everywhere, an epidemic that ravaged her community. Buildings were empty and burned out. They were either filled with drug dealers, addicts, or prostitutes selling their wares. Born and raised on the southside of Los Angeles, Enietra was no pushover. She knew how to handle herself, and she wasn't afraid of the streets. But she was also fun. Someone who could throw caution to the wind. So she decided: It couldn't hurt to get a ride to her friend's house. She opened the passenger door and hopped inside.

As he drove they bantered back and forth. He was funny and had an answer to everything. She matched him quip for quip. As he spoke, Enietra could feel her earlier sadness lift; she was actually having fun. In the spur of the moment, she invited the man to come to the party.

"I'll go," he said, turning his bespectacled face to Enietra.

The man drove down a side street, telling Enietra he had to get some money from his uncle before they could go to the party. He pulled the car up to the curb in front of an old, yellow house and, without saying anything, ran inside. Enietra tapped the car's upholstery, counting the moments, waiting for him to return. She didn't think anything of the brief stop. That was always the way it was with men. Always dropping something off or forgetting something. She would have patience for only so long. If he didn't come out soon, Enietra had thought, she would leave.

Finally, the guy exited the house and headed toward the car. As he opened the driver's door and slid inside, Enietra could immediately tell that something had changed. Gone was the flirty, coy man from minutes earlier. He now felt disconnected and cold as ice. His eyes had turned blank. He started the car and pulled away, staring straight ahead.

Shots Fired

Everything became quiet. Enietra could feel the pounding of her heart inside her chest. She wiped her hands on her miniskirt, contemplating her next move. Her palms had become sweaty. Her gut told her something was a little bit off with this guy. Why did she get into his car? His personality had changed too quickly. She didn't know what to do. Should she ask him to stop the car so she could get out and walk the rest of the way? Should she keep the peace until they arrived at her friend's house?

Enietra debated opening the passenger door and jumping out when the guy suddenly began to speak. He fired a slew of rapid insults at her, the words coming fast and furious. She barely had time to respond or gather her thoughts, but instinct pushed her defenses up. Way up. This was red-flag territory. No way was she going to let this fool treat her like this.

"Who do you think you are talking to?" she asked, her voice as tough as nails. She had her neighborhood querulousness and hoped he got the message that she wasn't a woman to mess with.

He didn't respond but instead pulled out a snub-nose handgun out of his jacket. He pointed the gun straight at her chest and without warning pulled the trigger. A loud crack filled the air as the bullet shot out of the handgun, hitting her square in the chest at point-blank range.

"You shot me!" Enietra screamed.

She looked down at the front of her white and blue peasant shirt. It was her favorite top to go out dancing in, and now she saw that the fabric was covered in dark red blood. She had an inane thought about never being able to get the stain out. But as the blood spread, she could make out a round bullet hole in the middle of her chest. Through the wound she could see the inside guts of her body. Enietra told herself, "Okay don't panic, don't panic. If you panic, you're a goner."

Before Enietra had a chance to make her next decision, her attacker pushed her back onto the passenger seat, climbed on top of her, and pulled up her miniskirt. Blood was spilling over the white seats, and she thought, "At least he won't be able to get away with it if the liquid stains the seats." Enietra was bigger and stronger than he was, but because she had so much blood coming out of her chest, she had no strength to resist.

He pressed his dry lips roughly onto hers. Enietra tried to move her face away, but he was persistent. He bore into her body.

"I'm bleeding. You shot me in the chest. Get off me!" Enietra yelled.

But he didn't listen. Instead, he pushed Enietra further back against the seat. She couldn't believe that this was going to be her demise. She turned her head and tried to search out the stars in the inky-black Los Angeles sky. A tear rolled down her cheek, suspended against her skin. Then she summoned some of her strength and kicked him hard, struggling to break free of his grasp. She grabbed the car's cold handle. It was so tightly shut, as if it was wedged into place, but she twisted and turned the metal as hard as she could. She struggled to get up and propel herself out of the car seat. The man grabbed her and pushed her back down. Enietra felt her momentary burst of power sap. But then he let go of her arms and a bright flash blinded her. What was that? Was he shining a flashlight in her eyes?

As the light illuminated the car, she could see her attacker's hands were occupied. It looked like he was holding a Polaroid, one of those newfangled cameras that were all the rage. It was big and bulky, and she was certain that was what it was.

Then the flash went off again.

He was taking pictures of her lying helpless against his car seat, bloodied and battered. She had enough strength left to lunge forward and grab the camera but her attacker easily pushed back.

He flinched at her surprise lunge. Her attacker thought she had given up. He began fiddling with the Polaroid, preparing to take more photos.

She couldn't worry about the camera a second longer.

Enietra knew this was her last moment to try and escape. Adrenaline flooded her body. She grasped at the door handle but it was slippery with blood, and her fingers couldn't get a grip on the knob. She clenched her fingers around the handle and pulled as hard as she could. Her attacker heard the sound. In a flash, he put down the camera, grabbed the gun, and began to beat her senseless. The cold steel smashed against her body and her skull. She could feel her bones crack against the insistent force. She held her arms against her head, huddling underneath their flimsy protection, trying to shield herself from the powerful blows raining down on her. Blackness was closing in on her, but she willed herself to remain conscious. If she passed out, she knew that meant certain death.

Then her attacker casually leaned her over and he opened the door a crack. She could hear the metal locks grind as they disengaged.

He kicked Enietra hard in her side, and in a flash, she tumbled out of the car onto the gritty pavement.

The orange Pinto remained frozen as the driver loomed over her, making sure Enietra's lifeless body remained crumpled on the ground.

Then, he started the car and sped off with a lurch.

After she could no longer hear the tires on the pavement, Enietra opened her eyes. The street was desolate, but she could hear some traffic noise nearby. But otherwise—silence. All the buildings and houses on the street were dark and sleeping. She didn't know where she was or where to go. Her entire shirt and skirt were covered in red, and stains smeared over her hands, hair, and face. Blood still flowed from the gaping hole in her chest.

Her heart was racing, and she could feel her strength fading.

Life had taught Enietra to help herself.

Rolling over, she used the edges of her elbows to push herself up. She could feel the gravel rocks push into her skin. Everything was slimy, and she kept slipping on blood slicks, but, eventually, through sheer determination, she rose to her feet. Like a zombie, she used her hands to guide her. She held them out in front of her and started to zigzag down the street. Weaving and unsteady, she soon realized she was walking down familiar roads. She wasn't that far from her best friend Lydia's house.

She continued to walk, leaving bloody smudges on the parked cars along the street. Then, right there in front of her was Lydia's house. Her vision blurry, she could make out lights in the two front windows, a beacon of hope, as she made her way onto the front porch, screaming her friend's name, "Lydia! Lydia!"

Enietra pounded on the sturdy door with the back of her fists but no one came to help. At her wits end, all energy exhausted, she sank onto the porch floor and blacked out.

Hunt for a Killer

It was just past 1 a.m. when Lydia arrived home to find her best friend lying in front of her house surrounded by a pool of blood.

When Enietra didn't show to go to the party, Lydia assumed it was because she didn't want to attend.

"He beat me with his gun," Enietra croaked to her friend before passing out once more.

Lydia went inside and confronted her petrified children as to why they didn't open the door. Huddling in their beds, they told their mother they were too scared when they saw the screaming woman covered in blood approach the house. They didn't recognize Enietra and were too nervous to let the unknown person inside the house. Lydia couldn't fault them. Seeing the state of her friend, she wasn't sure she would've unbolted the door either. She rushed toward the telephone. Enietra opened her eyes while Lydia was dialing 911.

A blue and white ambulance came screeching to Lydia's house, and paramedics loaded the beaten woman inside. It was the early morning of November 8, 1988, when paramedics rushed her into the emergency room of Harbor-UCLA Medical Center, a 570-bed public Los Angeles County teaching hospital located at 1000 West Carson Street in Torrance, California. They worked frantically to stop the blood from gushing out of Enietra's chest, as Dr. John Robertson, the doctor on duty, prepared to take her into emergency surgery. They needed to operate immediately if they were going to tie off her arteries, stop the bleeding, and save her life.

She had lost an enormous amount of blood, and they needed to stanch her wounds so she could survive. Before she went under the knife, Enietra calmly told the medical staff she had been shot point-blank by a stranger that raped her and tried to kill her. She wasn't going to let even a bullet in her chest stop this guy from getting away. Everyone needed to know what had happened so her attacker could be caught. The hospital staff called the Los Angeles Police Department and they came to investigate. The doctors were able to extract the damaged bullet lodged in Enietra's chest as evidence for the police.

A few days after her surgery, detectives were at her bedside to hear Enietra's story. Unbeknownst to her, a rash of similar attacks had been happening on the southside of Los Angeles. Maybe, the police surmised, they were connected to what had happened to this survivor. Exhausted and discombobulated from her experience, Enietra wanted to help the police catch the man who attacked her. She worked with the police sketch artist on a drawing. Even after the attack, her memory remained sharp and she was able to provide the artist with enough pertinent details to produce an accurate likeness of the madman. He was dark-skinned, with closely cropped hair and thick eyebrows shading light brown eyes. His image was distributed to police stations throughout Southern California. Patrol officers walked the streets, fliers clutched in their hands on the hunt for this elusive killer. Their suspicions that he was the perpetrator of other incidents continued to rise.

Police didn't tell Enietra that numerous other women had been murdered over the past few years. Their profiles had been similar to hers: young, black, and struggling with a range of problems from drugs to prostitution. The abductions happened in the middle of the night or in the early morning hours, when witnesses were scarce. All the women killed were from the southside of the city. As the body count began to mount, the community grew outraged, and groups formed demanding more answers. They started to put pressure on the LAPD to pay attention to their concerns.

Community leaders felt the police weren't seriously investigating these crimes. They grew frustrated that these women, whose lives often weren't valued, were getting murdered, and the police weren't making any progress. There was little evidence, few clues, and no eyewitnesses about who was targeting these women. Now, however, the police had something to start with—the ballistics from the bullet in Enietra's chest matched the gunshot wounds in the other dead girls. It was becoming clear the man who attacked Enietra was also their killer. Still, detectives didn't tell Enietra they believed her attacker was a serial killer.

A few days after the attack, detectives took her out to see if they could find the orange Ford Pinto she described. They drove the streets but didn't find a match. During the 1980s in Southern California, Pintos were a common sight. It seemed one was parked on every corner. But in all the cars they peeked into, none had the unique white seats. And, then, just like that, the killing stopped. With no further evidence and no more bodies found, the trail went cold.

Enietra tried to get back on her feet, all the while feeling that the police didn't trust what she told them. She confided to friends that the police behaved as though she were a prostitute or someone they didn't want to put the time and effort into. She felt demoralized. The more she tried to protest about the lack of attention to her case, the more she felt the detectives didn't believe her. She showed up at the police station. She asked the detectives where they were in their investigation. She tried not to get too upset; instead, she threw herself into her church and went back to school for a degree in medical assisting. She was determined to move forward with her life.

Thirteen Years Later

Thirteen years passed before the killer struck again. It was 2002 and, again, the police found the body of another young black girl, Princess Berthomieux, a runaway whose body was dumped on the southside. Two years later the body of 35-year-old Valerie McCorvey was discovered by a crossing guard. In 2007, 25-year-old Janecia Peters was found shot to death and covered with a garbage bag in an alley. This time, though, detectives had something that hadn't been possible all those years ago: DNA. Lab technicians were able to trace the DNA left on the bodies back to the murders that took place in the 1980s. It seemed the serial killer had awoken from his slumber.

Even though police had the serial killer's genetic profile, they still had no idea who he was. He wasn't listed in any of the criminal databases, which meant that, surprisingly, the killer had never been arrested or fingerprinted.

The LAPD formed a task force dedicated to hunting down the elusive murderer, but didn't alert the public of this new development. Within days, however, the *LA Weekly*, a local alternative paper, broke the story and nicknamed the serial killer "The Grim Sleeper" for his long drought between murders. A local councilman offered a $500,000 reward to the public in an effort to generate tips on the cold case. It was hard to get the general public interested in long-dead prostitutes, and barely any leads came in. The police pressed on. They hired a profiler to further understand the person they were hunting, and he was able to generate specific characteristics of the killer. In a 2009 press conference, Detective Dennis Kilcoyne, who had been on the case for years, announced a chilling prophecy. He said the suspect, probably in his fifties or late forties, was somebody that nobody would ever suspect—one of those types who would be described as a great neighbor.

In the meantime, Enietra's life was far removed from any of these new developments. She didn't even realize her case was related to the hunt for "The Grim Sleeper" until detectives approached her in 2006 at a laundromat with an array of mug shots. They told her about the new murders and explained they thought it was the same guy who shot her so many years ago. In that moment, she realized she was the only known survivor of a serial killer still on the loose. The detectives asked her to take a look at the photos to see if she recognized anyone from the array. She was in shock, but she didn't see any familiar faces in those photos.

Forensic techniques had advanced, and the likelihood they would catch the killer was greater than ever before. Using Enietra's 1988 sketch, the police released a composite drawing showing the suspected killer both as a young man and aged. They posted billboards around Los Angeles that promised rewards for information about "The Grim Sleeper." Police now wanted the public's help to catch this guy, a complete about-face from their earlier strategy. It seemed to be the only way to track the serial killer down.

Finally in 2010, using an emergency search warrant, police pushed down the door to a mint-green house, nestled on West 81st Street, where Lonnie Franklin, Jr., lived. Known as a beloved neighborhood fixture, Franklin was a retired garbage collector who was always willing to help others out; he would fix cars or help move a bedroom bureau. Neighbors knew him as someone with whom to drink a beer. He kept a supply of car parts stashed in his backyard, where neighbors could wrangle an old tire or rims for a quarter of the price they would pay at a garage. He lived with his wife of 32 years and doted on his grandchildren, who often came to visit.

But police were about to discover Franklin's darker side when they entered his house. They knew they had their killer after tracing his genetic code through a recent technique called familial DNA. Any family member who had a match to DNA of a person of interest—not just an exact match—would be explored further. Using this newly expanded search capability, police entered the DNA profile they had gathered from the past murders into the database and Franklin's son Chris, who was sitting in prison, convicted on drug charges, was a partial match.

Using Chris's DNA, the police started to investigate all his immediate family members, including Lonnie. It was a 100 percent match. The Los Angeles Police finally had their guy. During a three-day search through Franklin's house and workshop, detectives found hundreds of hidden photographs—almost 500 pictures—in addition to mementos from his crimes: pieces of jewelry and pornographic videos with footage of Franklin spliced inside. Wedged in the back of his workshop, in between two four-by-four pillars, the police found a Polaroid picture. It was of Enietra blacked out in the orange Ford Pinto on that fateful night so long before. Her eyes were closed, her shirt covered with blood. In the photo, she looked dead.

Reckoning Day

It was a warm summer day at the Los Angeles County Courthouse on August 10, 2016. Spectators shuffled back and forth, fanning themselves and uncomfortable in the stifling heat. They anticipated finally getting the satisfaction they had been awaiting for almost twenty-five years. After a three-month trial, a Los Angeles jury found Lonnie Franklin, Jr., guilty of ten counts of murder and one count of attempted murder for a series of killings spanning three decades. On sentencing day, before the judge pronounced his verdict, the only surviving victim and other victims' families were given the opportunity to speak to Franklin directly. The spectators listened expectantly as Enietra made her way to the lectern.

She said her name to the crowd and announced she was Franklin's only living victim. She expressed her sorrow and remorse for the families whose children didn't survive. Then she continued, "You are truly a piece of evil. You are right up there with Manson. And you did it to your own. I have fear of men who are supposed to care for me and protect me." She paused.

"You made me look at people differently," Enietra said to Franklin, turning to him. "But I'm still here."

In August 2016, Lonnie Franklin, Jr., was convicted of the murder of ten women and one attempted murder. Large gaps between Franklin's murders, which ranged from the 1980s to 2007, led the press to crown him "The Grim Sleeper." DNA samples taken from Franklin matched with traces of genetic material found on the women, and the ballistic evidence matched as well. Prosecutors said Enietra's story, as the only known survivor, helped convict Franklin for the other murders. Franklin was sentenced to death. He is currently on death row in California's San Quentin State Prison.

Mauro Prosperi
Run for Your Life
Marathon des Sables, Morocco, 1994

On the fourth day of the Marathon des Sables, a six-day, 156-mile endurance race in the Sahara Desert between Morocco and Algeria, a windstorm blew through the course. While training in Italy, Mauro Prosperi had heard about these infamous storms that could swoop into the desert on the spur of the moment. These freak weather incidents were uncontrollable, and organizers told the runners they had to prepare for any condition. Mauro had never experienced the desert before. He just knew it was one of the harshest environments on earth, so he could only imagine what the desolate lands would be like.

The landscape was so vast it was impossible to judge distance or separate one point from the next. During the marathon's first few days, most runners crossed from the third to the fourth checkpoint, with 57 miles stretching between them, the most brutal traverse of the race. At the Berber-style tented rest stops while peeling their socks off and tending to their pus-filled blisters, chatter between the athletes had provided endless horror stories about the first brutal length of track.

By the third day of the race Mauro knew he would have to muster all of his strength to keep his pace. This was the part of the course when many of the runners started to drop out or fall back, defeated by the undulating sand dunes and the sweltering sun. Mauro knew the day was going to be a huge challenge and a test of his stamina, but he had confidence in his athletic abilities. Although he had never run an extreme marathon before, he was in seventh place, ahead of many contestants with more years of experience.

The sky had been a startling azure on a hot, sunny day when Mauro had set off among the 134 other runners competing in this elite marathon. Music was blasting out of speakers positioned alongside the starting gates. Runners were dancing, bobbing, and laughing to the beat. There was a festive feeling in the air. Ahead of them lay the wild unknown of the Sahara Desert. The race required runners to be outside for days on end with nothing but sheer determination to pull them through. It was an intimidating and enormous mission.

Mauro's competitors were laughing and jostling, ready to start the event they had spent the last few months obsessively preparing for. Some of the competitors were experienced runners who had already participated in the marathon, happy to see old friends from around the world; others were there for the first time. The rush of adrenaline was universal.

Mauro felt good about his chances. Slim and lithe, with not one ounce of fat on his body, he had trained for months in Italy, running almost 40 miles daily, pushing himself to the brink. Sports had always been very important to him. As a former Olympic athlete, he had competed in the pentathlon, which consists of five different track and field events. He fenced, rode horseback, and ran great distances. At 39 years old, Mauro decided he needed a new challenge that could push him beyond his current routine. In passing, a friend had mentioned the idea of a long-distance endurance race. Mauro knew nothing about the Marathon des Sables, or the community of athletes participating, but he was drawn to the idea of pushing his limits.

Started ten years earlier, in 1984, the Marathon des Sables had attracted elite athletes from around the world, lured by the challenge of running through the unique terrain. Mauro wasn't any different, and the extreme conditions and unrivaled risks appealed to him.

The hardest part of the endeavor was convincing his beloved wife, Cinzia. With three young children—Silvia, Claudia, and Matteo—to care for, Mauro was employed as a full-time officer in the Italian police force. Cinzia was concerned he could get seriously injured, but he reassured her the worst that could happen was that he would "get a sunburn on his nose." In the end, she supported him, and when he set off to Morocco he had endured months of training and anticipation.

The heat was blistering, reaching almost 115 degrees by noon. He had a blue scarf wrapped around his head, and with his olive skin, dark eyes, and dark hair, Mauro could easily have been mistaken as a son of the Sahara. At an earlier checkpoint, Mauro had received his rationed two liters of water before heading out to the next stop. During the race, water was rationed quite severely, and runners seen drinking or taking more than their share of liquids were given a time penalty. At this point he was running well, toward the front of the pack, and he felt well hydrated. He only took a few small sips from his water bottle before continuing.

Because he was one of the leaders, race organizers weren't able to warn Mauro in time of an impending storm. And then out of nowhere, the winds suddenly came and whipped a wave of fine pieces of sand into the air, creating a blanket of dust so thick it became impossible to see. Mauro was passing small dunes when the storm started, and as his visibility became limited, he had no choice but to stop and crouch. He tried to stay in place as a yellow wall of sand came barreling toward him. Reaching into his knapsack, he pulled out a towel and quickly wrapped it around his face and nose, leaving just enough room to see and breathe. Mauro knew his predicament was dangerous—the sands could bury a man in minutes.

All Mauro was wearing was a pair of spandex running shorts and a thin running T-shirt. When he'd started the marathon, the conditions had been good.

By Mauro's watch, the storm lasted eight hours, and by the time the winds finally died down and the sand settled, it was already nighttime. Mauro wiped the layers of sand that had crusted over his face during the last few hours and peeled open his eyes.

The stars stood bright against the inky-black sky, and he was bitterly disappointed. Hours had passed since he'd been waylaid by the storm, and he knew there was no way he could catch up to the other runners. He felt as if he no longer had a chance of placing in the race. That was what he was most upset about in the moment. He didn't consider that he was stranded. He figured that upon first light, searchers would come and find him. The race was extremely well organized, and even though the marathon was an extreme test of endurance, only one runner had died during the history of the race—a young Frenchman who had had a heart attack.

Mauro decided to close his eyes for a few hours and get some rest. Even with a compass and map, he knew that trying to find his way in the desert at night was an impossible task. Mauro pulled out a lighter and his sleeping bag from his pack, and made a small campfire. He pulled the bag up to his neck, trapping as much heat as he could as the temperature dropped. As he drifted off to sleep, he could hear the scampering of desert mice as they burrowed in the sand near his feet. The wind whistled through his ears, a lonely howling sound reminding him that the Sahara was bigger and stronger than any man.

Lost in the Desert

When morning came, soft pink rays flooded the landscape, followed by the fireball of the sun rising over the dunes. The terrain Mauro had initially encountered was gone. During the night the dunes had shifted. In their place was a world he could barely recognize, and he had no idea where he was. Gone were the water tents and first aid stations he visited throughout the first three days of the race. Mauro didn't see any other runners around but thought to himself, "Sooner or later I will meet someone. There are so many people in my situation, I'm sure." With his foot he covered the remains of the campfire with sand and prepared his backpack. He began to run again, feeling his body ease back into a looping stride in the soft sand, confident he would see someone soon. But as the hours passed and he moved farther and farther into the desert without any signs of life, the first niggling seeds of doubt crept into his mind. "I'm lost," he thought. And then, most insistently, "I'm lost." The thought took over his mind, until he stopped running.

Mauro stood still. He was in shock. All the energy sapped out of his body as he surveyed the landscape—miles of rippling sand lay in front of him. There was no horizon. No familiar landmarks. He had no idea where he was or where to go. In just a moment he went from feeling confident and secure to realizing he was losing the specific senses he needed to survive. He had to be hyper alert and aware of the shifting desert.

From his backpack, Mauro dug out one of his stainless-steel water bottles and urinated into its empty chamber. When he'd packed his bag in Italy days earlier, he had prepared for every sort of emergency situation as directed by the race organizers. In his backpack was a subzero sleeping bag, compass, maps, packets of dehydrated food, water bottles, layers of clothing to manage the fluctuating desert temperatures, salt tablets, a small gas stove, and anti-venom medicine.

Race organizers had sent notices to all runners about how to prepare for the endurance race, cautioning them to take into consideration the weight and heft of the backpack they would have to carry for six days. The rules stipulated that the bag couldn't weigh less than 14.33 pounds or more than 33 pounds. The runners knew they had to carry all of their provisions, except for water, on their backs and weren't allowed to put down the bag once. It was their most important resource as well as their biggest curse. It was a matter of great consideration, and every athlete had their own strategy as they packed their bags. Mauro had carefully considered every item he put into his backpack.

He had balanced the number of items needed to successfully complete the race and tried to keep his pack light enough to carry. It had seemed he had more than enough as he'd hoisted on the pack at the starting line, knowing he would have to carry it for the entire race. But now it seemed painfully, woefully inadequate. Only one of his remaining bottles had a half-liter of water in it, and he didn't know when he would be able to refill it. That's why he decided to urinate right away. He knew his first urination was the clearest, and if he were forced to drink it later it wouldn't be as dirty or dangerous. He tried to gather his thoughts and use the compass and map for a general sense of direction. The best thing to do was to keep walking. If he stood still and waited, surely he would perish in the shifting sands of the desert.

Then he remembered the pamphlets that had been handed out upon registering, instructing the runners not to move if they got lost. It had said the race organizers would immediately send out extensive search parties, and the best thing to do would be for runners to stay in one place. They would surely get lost if they tried to get out of the desert on their own. He suddenly realized he had been making the wrong decisions. His pack by his side, Mauro promptly sat down on the top of a soft dune, scanning the horizon for any movement. As he waited, in the distance Mauro could hear a whirling noise. He shaded his eyes from the glare of the sun and looked up into the sky to see a black military helicopter scanning the horizon, searching for him. He waved his arms in the air and jumped up and down, but the pilots must not have seen him, as the helicopter veered away.

Unbeknownst to him, as soon as race organizers realized Mauro was missing, they had arranged for huge search parties. Employees were sent out in Range Rovers and given precise instructions to follow the directions runners took during the race. A pilot was hired to man a light aircraft over the desert sands, and volunteer foot searchers walked the trails calling Mauro's name. By the afternoon, when it became clear that Mauro was not going to be found, organizers called in the Moroccan military, which sent out helicopters and Berber trackers in a bid to find him. (In the Sahara, the goats were guided by nomadic Berber tribes who had lived in the desert for thousands of years, following their herds around through the sands. The Berbers dismantled their tents and built them up again in new locations.)

It was one of those choppers that flew near Mauro. As quickly as he could, he ripped open his backpack and pulled out his distress flare. He stuck the end of the red flare in the sand and lit one end. In a moment it set off, its plume of fire creating a trail in the sky before it petered out. He waited for the helicopter to spot the flare and turn back, but it didn't happen. The helicopter pilot didn't seem to have noticed Mauro's call for help even though he could see the outline of the pilot's head in the cockpit. He jumped up and down in the sand but, at the last moment, the helicopter banked right and maneuvered away from him. Its blades made a whirring sound as it pulled out of Mauro's sight. He was alone once more.

Mauro sat down in the sand, his head in his hands, despair coursing through his body. He crawled on the dunes holding his knife out in front of him, trying to stab scurrying beetles as they ran. The tip of his knife sank deep into the sand without getting his prey. Mauro screamed in frustration. Above him in the sky, two large scavengers flew, circling, as if searching for their next prey. Mauro knew he had to keep walking. If he just stood there, surely he would die; he would starve to death and his bleached bones would disappear underneath the desert sands.

After a couple of days of trekking, an image, or what he thought was an image, appeared in front of Mauro. As he grew closer he realized it was a cluster of Muslim shrines. These buildings were traditional rest stops where religious pilgrims relaxed as they crossed the Sahara. In front of him were three structures: a crumbling one-story brick building with a doorway that Mauro surmised was for lodging animals; a whitewashed brick building with a smaller front portico notched with three small windows and a brick pitched roof, where guests probably stayed; and a three-story brick tower dotted with windows. The tower seemed to be a lookout for passing travelers. Under the porticos travelers could gather shade, and drink and eat before continuing the treacherous journey. Mauro crossed into the cool, tiled shade of the white building providing cover from the relentless burning sun. He relaxed, exhausted by the strain of the past few days.

After he rested and regained a modicum of strength, Mauro decided to attach the red, white, and green Italian flag that he carried in his backpack to the top of the tower in case a helicopter flew past. He reasoned that if the search crew saw the flag, they would know he was either waiting there or had recently passed through. While climbing the narrow brick casement, he saw bats flying around the tower, their dark wings casting shadows on the ground. The noise of their screeching filled the air, and in the gloom, he could see their beady black eyes watching him. His hunger and thirst were intense, so in a flash, he decided to try and catch some of them. Grasping one hand tightly to the makeshift ladder, Mauro reached out and grabbed one of the bats. With a swift motion he pulled out his knife and slit open its body. Blood began to gush out, and Mauro held the small furry body to his lips, drinking in what he could. All he could taste was something warm and salty. He didn't want to think about the animal he was eating. He didn't want to vomit up the small amount of moisture and food he gained from the bat. He threw the spent body to the ground and as more bats flew by, he grabbed another, slit the body open, and drank again, until finally he felt satiated.

Emboldened by his success he scrambled down the tower, and he saw serpents and mice scattering in the recesses of the buildings. With his knife he stalked more prey, drinking the blood and eating whatever raw meat he could find.

Mauro fell asleep and woke up hours later after he heard the sound of an airplane overhead. He jumped up, heartened by the rumbling noise. They were still looking for him! It had been two to three days since he had seen those whirling helicopters, but then there had been silence. Mauro had started to think he had been abandoned. But up in the sky, hope sounded. He ran out to the dunes and with his hands wrote "S.O.S." in the sand, but within minutes, light winds had blown the sand back, covering any progress he had made with the letters. There had to be another way to attract the pilot's attention.

Mauro gathered any type of materials to bring to the shrine that would burn. He piled up some old papers, fabrics, and sticks and lit everything with the lighter and charcoal he carried in his backpack. The fire started to burn, but it was weak. The black smoke he envisioned would be big enough to alert the plane that he, Mauro, was still alive in the desert, failed to manifest. Sinking to his knees, Mauro felt despondent, knowing eventually the searchers would scale back their efforts and eventually begin to give up. They would never be able to find the remains of his body in the desert, and his family would have nothing to bury. "Maybe this was my destiny. I will die alone in the desert," he thought. Mauro contemplated killing himself. Even though he had drunk a lot of blood, he could feel his body weakening and he didn't want to die from dehydration. He'd heard stories that it was the worst way to expire, as it felt like strangulation. He became very frightened.

Soon though, he knew, his strength would diminish and he would die from thirst, starvation, or heat exhaustion in the harsh climate. He had gone almost six days without water, drinking whatever urine he could produce and the small amount of blood from the animals he was able to capture. But it wasn't enough. Whatever vigor he had left was quickly fading from his body.

Using a piece of charcoal from his earlier fire, he penned a letter to his wife, apologizing to her for doing the race and leaving their family in this way. He expressed his desire to have been a better husband and father. Satisfied that at least Cinzia and his children would know how much he loved them, he pulled his sleeping bag around himself. As he did so his wedding band slipped from his finger and fell into the sand. In an instant the gold ring tying him to his home and family had disappeared.

Mauro was devastated. He felt like this was a sign, so he decided to take his own life. It was better to die on his terms than to let the harshness of the Sahara take him with no dignity. With trembling fingers, he grabbed his knife from his shorts' waistband and began slashing himself across his arms and legs. He was too frail to make deep cuts, but the gashes split open, further weakening him, the blood spilling onto the floor in front of him. As he stared in disbelief, his head hanging over his knees, his eyes closed and he drifted off.

The Race Continues

Back at race headquarters, organizers decided to resume the marathon while they continued to search for Mauro. Participants were torn. They had spent months, even years training for this event, and thousands of dollars, but the thought of running while their colleague was somewhere slowly dying didn't feel right. But, they decided to continue, and four days after Mauro disappeared all the runners had crossed the finish line. However, there were no celebrations. The participants headed back to their home countries, still reeling from Mauro's disappearance. The Marathon des Sables had officially ended, but one of the runners was still unaccounted for.

In the meantime, Mauro's brother and brother-in-law, along with two Rome-based investigators from Interpol, the international police force, had arrived in Casablanca determined to assist with the search. Organizers hadn't immediately notified Cinzia, Mauro's wife, when he had gone missing. His family didn't know until a few days later, and they were understandably angry. They decided to form their own search party using European police.

Six days had passed since Mauro had disappeared and Moroccan officials didn't believe the runner was still alive. He didn't have any water and the desert reached triple-degree temperatures. No man had previously survived longer than four days in the Sahara without water. He had surely perished by now. Italian officials, however, couldn't be persuaded to give up so easily. Mauro was an athlete of some renown in Italy and a police officer, and there had been lots of media coverage when his family found out he was missing. The Italian government wanted to bring him home alive.

The next morning, rays of sunshine pierced Mauro's eyes, awakening him. Miraculously, he was still alive. Glancing down at his hands and legs, Mauro saw his wounds had begun to heal overnight and the blood had congealed and dried. All the cuts he had made to his wrist had closed and he was no longer losing any blood. He felt a glimmer of hope. Maybe it wasn't his destiny to die in the Sahara.

In a swift motion, Mauro leaned forward and grabbed a handful of sand where his wedding ring had slipped off the night before. As the sand sifted through his fingers, he could see the golden band shining in the center of his palm. He knew then it was time to leave the relative safety of the shrines and see if he could make it through the desert. He would survive after all, he decided all he had to do was to keep moving.

Mauro made a plan to stick to a strict routine. In his toughest moments, this had always gotten him through to a point of success. He would only walk in the early mornings and evenings, not in the harsh heat of the day. During the day he would rest in the shade of an occasional tree or in one of the caves that dotted the landscape. He used his compass and thought he was heading east, but wasn't sure, as the surroundings morphed. The days started to blend together, and there was no way for him to tell how long he had been in the Sahara.

Mauro knew the most important thing was access to liquids. He needed to keep hydrated and conserve his energy. In the mornings he licked dew from the rocks, which had collected overnight when the temperature dropped. In his backpack, he found a packet of wet wipes, and every hour he sucked on a small corner of a wipe, regenerating the saliva in his mouth and bringing moisture to the back of his throat. There were only a few more wipes left in the packet. At night Mauro would dig a hole in the sand and get into the sleeping bag, then jump into the hole and pile all the heavy sand on top of him. It was the only way that he could keep himself warm enough throughout the frigid desert nights.

As he continued walking, he decided to leave traces behind and dropped inconsequential items along his path hoping searchers would find them. First, he left a shoelace, next a pair of socks, then a tube of tinfoil. Finally, he started balling up tinfoil torn from his food containers, leaving the shiny clues behind, glinting in the sun. He fashioned a slingshot from a stick he found in a cave and used his knife to kill a snake, shoving any type of protein or liquid into his mouth, no matter what it was. As he was losing his strength, he was gaining something else: a hyperawareness he had never experienced before. He felt every movement; every hidden jewel of the desert revealed itself to him. Mauro had never felt more alive.

The days passed, but still, Mauro didn't lose hope. He was sure he would make it out of the Sahara. He understood the desert now—all his experiences had led him to moments of truth, and he would survive.

While walking, Mauro thought he saw the shimmer of water ahead of him. He squinted and peeled back the scarf wrapped around his face. Was it a mirage? Nine days alone in the desert had begun to play tricks on his mind. There were several times he thought he had seen food or his family, only to realize the desert had deceived him. Using a burst of strength, he ran up to the water and saw it was just a muddy puddle. But it was liquid. Easing himself onto his stomach, Mauro cupped his hands and took a sip. He tried to take a gulp, but realized he couldn't open his mouth to swallow. The cool water slid down his throat and, almost immediately, he vomited. Mauro lay on his back, staring up at the sky. Finally, he'd found water, but he couldn't even drink it.

After a few moments, he forced himself back onto his stomach and scooped up enough for a tiny sip, forcing the liquid down the back of his throat. He closed his mouth, and waited. The liquid stayed in his stomach. A few moments later he took another swig. Over and over, Mauro sipped the water until his thirst had abated. It must have taken him hours to drink his fill, because the sun was overhead in the middle of the sky when he finished. He didn't want to get caught in the heat and needed to get to some shade. As he filled his water bottle, he thought there were sure to be animals or an encampment nearby. An oasis in the Sahara was a rare thing, and Mauro knew there had to be more.

As he scanned the terrain, his hunch was proven correct when he saw a few goats milling around, heading toward the watering hole. Mauro knew where there were goats, there had to be shepherds. The animals were far too valuable to wander alone in the desert.

Sure enough, a young shepherd girl in a long robe appeared moments later. She looked to be about eight years old, the same age as one of Mauro's three children. She whistled to the animals, seemingly not noticing him until he started walking toward her. As Mauro approached, the girl screamed in fear and ran off disappearing over the sand dunes. He must have looked like a skeleton. He could only imagine what a fright his appearance gave the young child.

Mauro tried to speak, to calm her, but she ran away too fast. He followed her over the sand dunes and saw she had run into a cluster of tents erected in a semicircle around a campfire under a cluster of trees. Berber women swarmed outside to see the crazed man the girl was jabbering about. As soon as they saw the condition Mauro was in—famished and nearly blinded by nine days in the harsh sun—they weren't frightened. They could see he was badly injured. The Berber women offered Mauro some goat's milk, which he drank greedily. When they offered him an array of food, he took small pieces, chewed them slowly, and then promptly threw up.

In that moment, Mauro understood that he was saved.

During the 1994 Marathon des Sables, nine days passed before Mauro Prosperi was rescued from the wilds of the Sahara. He had strayed 180 miles off course from the race and crossed the border twenty-five miles into Algeria. He lost almost thirty-three pounds and was severely dehydrated. It took Mauro almost two years to fully recover from his injuries. Four years later, Mauro Prosperi returned to Morocco, where he competed in the marathon for the second time. He dropped out due to a stubbed toe. In 2012, on his third attempt, he finally completed the race.

Coach Ek and the Wild Boars Soccer Team

One for the Team

Tham Luang Cave System, Thailand, 2018

During the dry season, the national park was frequented by adventurers and cyclists exploring the rocky terrain, clear grottos of the stunningly beautiful, lush mountain landscape, and Thailand's fourth-largest cave system. But in the rainy season, most locals knew to steer clear of the rocky outposts and intricate system that made up the Tham Luang caves, as people had gone missing within their murky depths.

The youth from the local soccer club had been ready for an adventure. After an intense period of practice, their assistant coach had promised them an hour of spelunking and exploring in the Tham Luang Cave system. The day had started out carefree, as a group of teammates cycled through forested green hills, past flooded rice fields to the caves' entrance, excited by the fun ahead. The newest team members were to hike as far as possible through the cave system's tunnels to write their names on the walls. It was a time-honored initiation that every new teammate of the local outlet, The Wild Boars, accomplished.

Coach Ek, the group's leader, brought along supplies he anticipated they would need for their excursion: a flashlight, spare batteries, and a rope. The boys planned to only stay at the caves for an hour or so, long enough to have some fun and leave before it turned dark. They didn't have much time because their mothers wanted them to be home for dinner. Most of them were teenagers or younger, ranging in age from eleven to seventeen years old. And for all but two of the boys and Coach Ek, they had never been to the caves before.

The boys worshipped their leader, who, at just twenty-five years old was dedicated to the local boys who played on the youth soccer team. "He has a beautiful heart," the boys would say about Ek.

Ek had overcome great obstacles in his short life as a member of the ethnic group Tai Lue. As minorities, the Tai Lue, who maintained their own dialect and lived on the outskirts of Thai society, weren't allowed to obtain identity cards, which ensured they struggled to gain a foothold in employment and schools. Coach Ek's parents had died when he was just a 10-year-old boy, and he was sent to a Buddhist temple to be raised by monks. Three years before he'd joined the coaching team of the Wild Boars, he'd left the temple, but as a former monk, he still had an aura of calm that made parents comfortable. He always thought of activities for the children and made sure they were set into motion. The boys blossomed under his careful tutelage.

Into the Caves

As the boys investigated the network of tunnels, running and laughing through the narrow passageways, it started to rain outside. They could hear drops hitting the rocks as a sudden heavy, blinding storm pummeled the area, filling the cave system with water. They'd expected storms to hit at some point. During monsoon season, the skies opened and closed, dumping large amounts of rain but also providing sunny respites.

It was the way of life during Thailand's monsoon season, and they didn't want the weather to deter them.

The sprawling cave system, which straddles Thailand and its neighboring country Myanmar, is a complex system of tunnels running approximately six miles. Inside, the caves consist of narrow corridors, which traverse underneath the length of the mountainous ridge. The rough tunnels dip and climb at various points; there are places where climbers have to crawl on their stomachs and others where they can walk upright. The tunnels connect to cavernous limestone rooms dripping with stalactites. Day trippers often come to see one of the larger areas called Pattaya Beach, named after a popular tourist beach south of Bangkok.

Reaching this chamber was a two-mile hike from the entrance, and along the way there were a number of smaller chambers where climbers could swim and sit on the sandy ledge. Halfway through the hike there was an intersection where many climbers stopped to rest, as traversing the walkways could take up to a few hours. To the right of this intersection was a tunnel that led to Pattaya Beach, its limestone path well-worn by years of thrill-seeking visitors.

The boys wanted to try and make it to the famed Pattaya Beach and urged Ek to lead them to the sandy crest. As they ran deeper through the tunnels toward their destination, they played and called to each other. Suddenly, with a roar, a flash flood brought an avalanche of water into their area. Swirling muddy water filled with twigs filled the tunnels, reaching their chests.

The boys had to scramble farther into the caves, running away from the onslaught of water. As they saw the liquid approach, fear pounded inside their chests, as most of the boys didn't know how to swim. Adrenaline set in and the boys pumped their legs until they were able to reach a wide, beach-like area where there was room for all twelve of them, plus Coach Ek, to sit. The flood had come so suddenly there was hardly any time to react much less escape via the front entrance, which now seemed miles away. The turbid water that rushed into the tunnels was mixed with mud and branches, completely blocking their exit.

After a few hours the water subsided a bit, but didn't recede enough for the team to leave. Coach Ek decided to test the possibility of leaving the cave system through the passage in which they'd entered. They boys had already made their way deep into the system and didn't even know how far from the main entrance they were. There was the possibility they had walked too far to find their way back.

"I'm scared," said 13-year-old Mongkol Boonpiam. "I'm afraid I won't get to go home and my mom will scold me," he said.

Ek told the boy that he was going to find a way out of there, but first needed to understand how far in they were.

He wound a length of the rope around his hand, and asked three of the boys to hold on tight to the other frayed end while he dived into the flooded tunnel.

"If I pull the rope twice, you need to pull the rope back in and get me back to the ledge, because it means I have no oxygen," he said. The boys agreed and held tight to their end as Coach Ek lowered himself down into the muddy water. Taking a deep breath, he ducked his head under and swam toward the opening. Wide-eyed, the boys watched anxiously; however, within moments, Coach Ek realized he wouldn't be able to make it through and yanked twice on the rope. Using all their strength, the boys strained to pull him back from the swirling water.

Finally Coach Ek climbed soaking wet back onto the ledge. In the boys' eyes, Coach Ek could see they knew they were in more trouble than they earlier realized. It wasn't possible just to return to the front of the cave, pick up their bicycles, and ride home for dinner.

Coach Ek squared his shoulders. He was the only adult there and the boys were his responsibility. He had to do everything in his power to keep them calm and their spirits up while they waited to be rescued. He was confident that soon enough families would realize the boys were missing and would send help.

It had been raining steadily, and as the hours passed, day turned into night without the boys arriving home, and their families grew concerned. They knew where the boys were, as their excursion had been discussed on a group WhatsApp chat, but a few hours after the boys left, the first worried text popped up from a parent wondering what time the boys would be home. As they texted each other back and forth, some of the parents decided to head to the caves to make sure the boys weren't still inside. In front of the cave entrance, they found their sons' bicycles and some discarded sneakers, but no signs of their children. Their worst fears were confirmed. The boys were still inside the caves.

A Global Rescue Effort

By the following day, Thai Navy SEALs arrived at the caves after villagers notified government authorities, realizing they couldn't retrieve the boys on their own. Night had already fallen by the time the SEALs arrived to assess the scene. They were hopeful that the boys had made it to Pattaya Beach, which would give them a good chance of survival because the ground is high, with porous openings leading to the outside so the boys could have access to oxygen and a supply of fresh water from the underground springs. As long as the team stayed put for a few days in that location, the SEALs were confident, they would be able to rescue them.

That night, SEAL divers prepared for their first submersion into the murky waters to search for the boys. The conditions were rough and the mud-filled waters were rising quickly, making it close to impossible to make any progress through the tunnels. SEAL divers advanced in teams of three, but shortly conditions forced them to ascend after only small bursts of exploration. The tunnels were too flooded to do a more extensive search. The government decided to bring in submersible pumps to try and drain the flood waters from the inundated chambers. They also sent climbers overland through the dense jungle looking for any entryways to the network of caves below. It was a fruitless pursuit, however, as they couldn't find any clear openings through which to enter.

Two days after the boys were trapped in the caves, the Thai government asked for help from technical experts from various countries around the world. Military personnel, from British diving experts to American survival specialists, were ready to assist in the rescue. The Thai Navy SEALs had been able to establish a command center in a section of the cave about a mile from the main entrance. It served as a "war room" for all the technical experts. Maps were plastered along the walls, showcasing the cave's extensive network of arteries, and a state-of-the-art communication center was hoisted through a dry passageway. There, rescuers plotted ways to find the boys before time ran out. Helicopters equipped with heat sensors and drones with thermal cameras whirled overhead, searching for any access points in the terrain.

The cameras created an aerial map with 3D images of the search area. The sensors were able to detect what searchers couldn't see through the blinding rains that continued to batter the area: There were two possible locations to enter the caves. One was from up above, a few hundred feet from the entrance, and the other was through a small room about 40 meters from Pattaya Beach, where the rescuers hoped the boys were still alive.

Inside the cave, Coach Ek crossed his arms and legs in a lotus shape and encouraged the boys to do the same. He drew from his experience in the temple, where he was able to calmly meditate for hours on end. The boys mimicked their mentor and slowly breathed in and out, trying to keep themselves from panicking. During their meditation sessions, Coach Ek taught them to breathe in as little air as possible, understanding that the oxygen pockets within the caves were limited and rapidly decreasing.

Each day they carved out time to meditate. Not only did it help the boys relax and focus, but it brought them closer.

At night, the boys hugged each other to ward off hypothermia, as nightly temperatures in the caves dropped below freezing. In the beginning of their ordeal, the boys would turn their flashlights on and off, chasing away the shadows, but as time wore on, they left their lights off in an effort to conserve their limited batteries. Using pointed rocks, the boys kept themselves busy during the endless days by digging into the cave walls, searching for a way out.

"We took turns. That was our routine for ten days," said Coach Ek.

Coach Ek rationed out the meager amount of food they had with them, often choosing to go without so the boys would have enough to eat. After a few days, their food had run out, but there was plenty of water dripping from the cave's enormous stalactites and burbling through the springs. Cupping their hands, the boys drank as much water as they wanted. Still, the team's hunger increased and a pervasive darkness was closing in on them. Coach Ek was growing nervous as he saw the boys becoming gaunter. Fresh air seeped through the porous limestone, keeping them alive, a reminder of the outside world.

Making Contact

Nine days after the soccer team disappeared into the intricate cave system, divers found them alive, perched on an elevated ledge above the encroaching water. The divers had been searching the area for days, and only a few hundred meters from where the team was marooned, they got lucky and found an air pocket. When they surfaced into an impenetrable darkness, they had to use their noses to smell for any signs of human life and had a feeling the boys were close by.

"We smelled the children before we saw or heard them," a diver named John said.

The team had ventured almost two-and-a-half miles into the tunnels, much farther than Pattaya Beach, where they were thought to be. Yet their distant location had been advantageous for their survival. The rock they were sitting on was raised high enough that the boys were able to derive enough oxygen from the porous limestone. They were still alive and, more surprisingly, they were dry, but some were suffering from hypothermia. Rescuers had to swim nearly four hours to reach their location, gliding through treacherous waters with zero visibility.

After the boys were found, the Thai government worked to figure out a way for them to communicate with their families and the rescuers. Divers attempted to weave fiber-optic cables through the tunnels, but their efforts didn't work. In the end, the kids communicated with their parents by writing letters. In the ensuing days, divers took batches of letters from the boys out of the caves and to their families, the precious papers kept dry in waterproof capsules.

"Mom and Dad please don't worry. I will get out soon and help you at the shop," one of the boys wrote in a heartfelt plea to his parents.

"When I get out can you take me to the pan-fried noodle shop?" wrote another on the lined school notebook paper.

"I'm fine, but it's a little cold. Don't worry, and don't forget my birthday!" implored another boy. Parents were thrilled to hear from their children after long days filled with torment.

Divers also brought in easy-to-digest foods and vitamins so the boys could maintain their strength. The boys showed good humor and an upbeat attitude, encouraged by their coach, who had been a bedrock for them during the ordeal.

A Nation on Edge

Now, the rescue team had to figure out how to get the twelve boys and their coach out of the caves alive. Rumors started to circulate in the press. Thai newspapers carried reports that rescuers couldn't attempt a rescue until the rainy season passed—at least four months in the future. Television networks broadcasted that the waters in the caves were rising, and the boys wouldn't be able to survive another few days. Foreign news outlets from around the world besieged Thailand, captivated by the heroic tale of the stranded team. Glued to their televisions, the public watched step-by-step reports of whether the soccer team could be brought to safety. It was constant chaos, and no one, not even the divers waiting, knew what would happen.

The nation was on tenterhooks and people wanted to help in any way that they could. Outside of the caves, interspersed with the media scrum, Thai locals cooked for rescuers and volunteers. Thailand's king sent food, supplies, and funds to assist the rescue team, while supporters prayed around the clock. Everyone was coming together with the common goal of saving the boys.

Rescuers were anxious to go into the chambers to extract the team. They were tired of waiting for the right moment, but the eyes of the world were on them, and there couldn't be any mistakes.

The water level continued to rise, and soon it would overtake the ledge where the boys were waiting. It was finally time to launch the rescue operation. On July 10, 2018, the boys had been in the caves for almost two weeks, there was a break in the weather and the rain subsided. Now was the rescuers' chance to get all of the children.

During the last few weeks, monsoon storms had pelted the area, and on that day the locals predicted the caves could be completely flooded once the rains started again. The trapped boys would surely drown. The Thai government needed to act immediately.

The pressure on Thailand's Navy SEALs was immense. On July 6, they'd already lost one of their own. Diver Saman Gunan had died during an overnight operation delivering extra air tanks to the cave. SEAL divers remembered him as they prepared to recover the children. The entire world was counting on them to succeed.

Before they started their operation, rescuers had practiced diving with children in local pools, practicing swimming with them in their arms. The plan was to use divers to guide the boys through the tunnels to the entrance. Even though the boys weren't experienced divers and were weakened from their lack of food and water, experts decided there was no other way to bring them out safely. Engineers planned to pump out water from the cave system, creating dry air pockets for the boys to periodically take breaks on their way out of the tunnel. All coordinates had been triple checked, and the rescue needed to happen.

There were nearly 150 Thai and foreign divers on standby waiting to rescue the boys. During the planning of the operation, overseas military operations provided search-and-rescue equipment, but there still wasn't enough gear to go around for all rescuers. Some of the divers had to wear makeshift gadgets secured by duct tape. Once enough water was pumped out of the tunnels and levels sank low enough, it was time to begin the operation.

Rescued

"Let's go!" When the authorities said to move, there was no hesitation.

The rescuers decided to take the boys out of the cave in small groups. In the first phase of the operation, the divers took out four boys. The journey was perilous, and the first group was in a sense, the guinea pigs.

The boys were ferried out, supported by two divers each, with the first team leaving the cave between 5 and 6 p.m. and the second between 7 and 8 p.m. In the hours before the undertaking, crews worked frantically to pump out as much water as possible from the caves. Their hard work brought a measure of success—some areas of the caves were walkable, although most of the route remained underwater. Since many of the teens were not strong swimmers and some had never previously dived, rescuers gave the children medication to relieve their anxiety before entering the water. For most of the passage, the boys were sedated by the drugs, some fully unconscious.

Each of the boy's faces was covered with a full mask, which was pumped full of oxygen. American navy divers brought special masks to the mission, but soon realized they only had adult sizes. With the help of local children and a swimming pool, the masks were tested and retrofitted. After a combination of straps and tightening, the masks fit securely on the local children's faces. The greatest test of all came when the divers pulled the masks onto the sleeping boys and lowered them into the water.

From the initial rescue point, divers had to navigate the treacherous journey in two primary sections. Guide ropes had been hung in the air chambers so the pair of divers accompanying each child could be directed through the most dangerous sections. The tunnels were so narrow that only one diver could fit through at a time, pushing their hands against the rocky outcrops to propel them through the swirling water. At other points, rescuers had to haul the boys up a steep incline using improvised pulley systems. There were long sections to traverse underwater, sometimes for up to an hour during the eleven-hour journey. Stationed at different points in the tunnels—holding lamps and torches—were various medical staff, doctors, and nurses who checked the boys' pulses and general condition.

Each child had a tank of air strapped in front of them and a handle tied to their backs, which the divers, whose teeth were chattering from the cold, used to maneuver the children through the bends in the tunnels. The boys were held facedown so the water rushed past their faces. In extremely narrow sections, the rescue teams had to stop to unstrap their own air tanks and then swim through the difficult points unprotected, without letting go of the boys. For even the most experienced divers, being without air for a few minutes in the water was a severe risk, but one they were willing to take to save the children.

It took hours for the divers to reach the midway point with the first group of boys. The divers climbed out of the water, pulling the boys behind them, but there was no cause for celebration. Phase two was still ahead, and this part of the passage was longer and more arduous than the previous one. The boys were placed inside a bendable, plastic stretcher, which partially cocooned them from the sharp rock edges and frigid waters. Then, a team of five divers hoisted the stretcher onto their shoulders and entered the water. The boys were suspended above the surface and the stretchers were able to float in the narrower parts, propelled forward by the divers swimming underneath. Along the way were containers of oxygen for the divers to refresh their air tanks.

The first evening, four boys had been rescued from the caves and taken to the hospital. A few hours later, they were requesting their favorite foods.

The world cheered.

But the work had just begun. Exhausted divers had to rest after the first rescue phase and resupply in preparation to bring out the next group. The weather forecast had predicted an impending storm, so they needed to go back in before all the passageways were flooded again.

The next morning, once all the oxygen tanks were refilled and assembled, divers moved in for their second rescue attempt. They took out four more boys, tracing the route they had used the day before. All four were taken out of the caves safely and whisked off to the hospital.

"We weren't sure if it was for real," 14-year-old Adul Samon told reporters when he was rescued.

The next day it was time for the third and final expedition. The rescue team was under immense pressure. This time, they had to take out the four remaining boys and Coach Ek, who wanted to be the last person to leave. The whole nation was waiting expectantly for the coach who had selflessly protected and saved the boys.

During the final rescue, one of the divers lost his grip on the ropes guiding the group through the darkness. The expedition froze; the rescuer needed to find the rope before the rest of the team could move forward. While holding onto one of the boys, the diver slowly moved backward down the tunnel, retracing his steps, hoping he could retrieve the rope, and finally picked it up. After seventeen days of working to rescue the boys, they were steps away from completing their mission. Anticipation rose in the air as the divers waded through the final section of the cave to the outside world.

Later that evening, the last group of boys, along with Coach Ek, emerged from the caves to cheering throngs.

Their ordeal was over.

The twelve members of the Wild Boars soccer team and their coach survived seventeen days inside the Tham Luang cave system. After their rescue, the boys were quarantined in the hospital for weeks, but suffered few physical repercussions from their time underground. Numerous books and movies have been made about their miraculous rescue.

Josiah Mitchell
On the High Seas
Sinking of The Hornet, *Pacific Ocean, 1866*

"Load the lifeboat with supplies!" the ship captain yelled over the din of the raging fire. He watched the crew as they rushed around the deck gathering their personal belongings and food reserves to take into the descending boats.

The Hornet had been burning all night. Bursts of white-hot flames shot from the depths of the ship's belly, licking the wood from the steerage to the deck. Embers devoured the stitched linen sails, which had hung so proudly just a few hours earlier on sturdy wooden masts. The fire had started the previous morning on Thursday, May 3, 1866, and it had been burning for twenty-four hours straight.

By 9 o'clock that morning, the mast had fallen and Captain Josiah Mitchell knew his ship wouldn't be able to sail any longer. All their efforts to stanch the fire had failed. As the crew poured bucket after bucket of water over the fire, the flames burned even higher.

He knew there was little chance of survival if they stayed on the ship. Josiah gave the signal to lower the lifeboats into the choppy sea.

Doomed Voyage

Josiah couldn't believe the bad luck *The Hornet* had been having from the beginning of its voyage. This was one of the worst expeditions he'd ever taken, and Josiah had been on many. The beginning of the journey was pleasant enough, and the weather had been steady since leaving the winter behind. The men were bored when they rounded the tip of Cape Horn, but shortly afterward things had started to turn south. They had struggled through bouts of bad weather since leaving the East Coast, and for weeks it seemed the gloom wouldn't lift. Rain and cold bashed the ship, and the crew spent most days in the dark, huddled inside. Tempers had been growing short. There seemed to be no end in sight, but then, after rounding the seas to head up toward California, the weather started to improve, shifting the men's moods.

After months of being cooped up, the crew was glad for the fresh air. It seemed as if the troubles in the beginning of the voyage had faded away—then, the fire happened. Combined with the crew's ongoing dysentery and sickness, Josiah felt a pang of relief abandoning *The Hornet*. Maybe the ship was cursed. He had never had this type of difficulty during any of his voyages, and he struggled with mixed emotions of guilt and disgust.

Twenty years of experience navigating the open sea and soon he was going to end up on a triad of lifeboats with a gaggle of men he didn't like very much and an expedition he didn't believe in. Josiah hadn't felt confident about commanding *The Hornet* since signing on for the voyage from New York to the Sandwich Islands. (In 1866, Hawaii was still known as the Sandwich Islands, and the atolls were populated by a mix of indigenous people and incoming adventurers.) He'd agreed to helm the ship after receiving a telegram at 4 a.m. accompanied by a letter from a former employer, Captain Prince Harding, asking him to come aboard. Josiah didn't feel he had the luxury of saying no. Captain Harding had gotten him the helm of many ships over the years, and he knew he couldn't afford to decline an offer. As a man of fifty-three, Josiah felt he might not get another chance to captain a ship, though quite frankly, he wasn't sure he could even handle the rigors the trip demanded. Responsible for transporting cargo from New York Harbor to San Francisco before heading to the islands, he knew the voyage would traverse rough oceans, most of it without land in sight.

Josiah had agreed on the princely sum of $200 per month for the duration of the voyage, a healthy amount he could use to support his wife and daughter. His wife suffered from an illness that required around-the-clock care and kept her bedridden in New York City. He didn't want to shirk his financial duties, even though he was off traveling for most of the time he had been married. A serious man with thick brown hair, piercing blue eyes, and a robust brown beard, Josiah had been sailing on merchant ships since he was barely out of his teen years. His whole adult life he had spent on ocean voyages. For months at a time he walked the decks, steering ships safely into various world harbors. It was the only way he knew how to support himself and he loved the work.

Two weeks after receiving the telegram notifying him of the Hornet position, Josiah set sail. It was the depths of winter, and ice was still clogging the choppy harbor waters. Josiah had to use his best navigation skills to safely maneuver the ship from between the wooden docks of the city's harbor through its treacherous mouth. Days earlier, a dangerous Nor'easter storm had blown into the East Coast, a combination of gale winds and sleet covering North Carolina to Nova Scotia in a blanket of ice and snow.

Henry Ferguson, one of the ship's two passengers, along with his brother Samuel, had booked passage on the Sandwich Islands–bound vessel so his brother's health could be mended by the tropical air. Dressed in a black suit with a blue wool overcoat, gloves, and bowler hat, Henry leaned against the boat's railing watching the hull cut through the black ice of New York Harbor. He wasn't sorry to leave the cold, busy city behind. He loved the frenetic energy of New York, but the glacial winters had left a bitter taste. He only hoped the voyage would lead to a new life for him, and that his brother's life would be revitalized with the change in weather and climate.

Samuel's health had suffered terribly in the time they had spent in the city. Henry's once robust, strapping brother was now a pale image of his former self. Henry worried incessantly about his brother's well-being, as it was he who'd brought him to New York, lured by promises of wealth and culture. Henry had decided he was going to be the one to fix his brother's troubles. *The Hornet* was going to take the brothers through the first half of their journey. They planned to stop at San Francisco, which Henry hoped would provide the culture that Samuel desired in the new city. Henry wanted to see his brother settled and at peace before he returned east, where he planned to return to continue their business ventures. Hopefully, once everything was settled there, he would travel between the coasts.

The ship's planned route was to sail south in the Atlantic parallel to the coast of Africa, around Cape Horn, back north through the Pacific off the coast of Mexico, then out to the Sandwich Islands. Josiah prayed the clipper would make it all the way, as these were rough waters they had to sail through. He had major concerns, as the ship wasn't in first-class condition. When he first inspected it, he'd noticed rotting wooden boards, cases of food stashed from eons ago, and termites in the hold. He should have delayed the launch in order to fix all the issues with the ship, but the crew had already been paid and were on board, ready to set off. They were getting restless, and Josiah knew there was nothing worse than an unhappy crew. If they dry docked, the crew would start womanizing and boozing, and that would delay their schedule. Merchants had paid top dollar to send their goods to the communities settling in the West. The 1,428-ton ship was filled to the brim with coal, iron, 6,200 boxes of candles, 2,460 cases of kerosene, and other miscellaneous products.

And now Josiah's worst fears were materializing: His lifeboats were lowered. Abandoning ship was a last-case scenario. Once they left the relative safety of the large vessel, they would be fairly unprotected from the wild seas. He was hoping that nearby ocean carriers would see the smoke and circle around to pick up the crew.

Fire in the Hold

Josiah wanted to be able to ferret out how the fire had originally gotten started before he put the lifeboats down. Rumors circulated that a disgruntled crew member had gone into the bowels of the ship with an open lamp to take some varnish from a large vat. The story Josiah eventually got from the crew was that the questionable mate fetched the varnish straight from the hold. Unfortunately, this had been a terrible mistake. The torch he was holding tipped into the barrel, igniting the highly flammable varnish.

"Help! Bring water!" the mate had frantically called as the fire quickly spread.

Other crewmen barreled toward the hull, the front part of the ship that floats on the water, when there was an explosion, pushing everyone back from the fiery area. They'd watched, helpless, as the flames leapt from the varnish and subsequently set fire to the extra sails stored in the lockers that lined the wooden hull.

As the fabric from the sail disintegrated, pieces broke off and dropped to the floor, starting a chain of flames that rapidly traveled through the ship.

"Fire! Fire!" a seaman screamed, running up to the deck to alert the others. The mate who'd started the fire stayed below, trying to put out the increasing flames with thick woolen blankets he had ripped off the beds of the three sick men in the infirmary. The men cowered in their naked beds, unable to leave due to illness. They most likely went down with the ship.

"Close the hatches!" Josiah shouted in the ensuing panic.

But it was too late.

The extra sails that were supposed to be for the lifeboats, most of the ammunition, and the medicine went up in flames. The alarm bells started to ring. Smoke began to billow so thick it was hard to see through the dense curls.

There was no longer any reason to stay on *The Hornet*. No other ships or search lights approach. Josiah knew they were battling a lost cause. They would never make it off the ship alive if they didn't leave immediately.

"Onto the lifeboats," Josiah ordered his thirty-three crew members. Scrambling, they untethered rickety boats, which were filled with as many provisions as possible.

The men had loaded royal sails, which were studded with grommets, into each boat. These sails were harder to lift and hoist, and didn't catch the wind as well, but they were all they had left in case they needed to change the mast. Provisions were divided among the three boats. They had managed to salvage four hams, twelve tins of assorted meats, a box of raisins, seven pieces of pork, a four-pound keg of butter, one hundred pieces of bread, and four buckets of raw potatoes.

Josiah had the men load twelve gallons of water and the ship's navigations instruments, including a chronometer, which determined longitude, compasses, and a quadrant, which measured latitude while at sea. On the positive side, they were able to secure a 100-pound drum of good-grade tobacco and some pipes and matches. Woolen blankets were thrown into the boats, but the men took no extra clothes. All they had to wear was the clothes on their backs. Most were outfitted in filmy linen trousers and open-necked shirts. The fabric didn't provide much protection.

Two of the lifeboats were small, and there was one larger vessel, a longboat. Nine men were assigned to each of the smaller boats, and fifteen to the longboat, two of whom were Henry and Samuel Ferguson. In his journal, Henry noted that the boats were lowered into the water at 6 p.m.

Josiah had divided the crew by their abilities, so there were enough men who could navigate, others who knew how to use mapping instruments, those who knew how to cook, and so on. Josiah himself went into the longboat alongside the two paying passengers, the third mate, and eleven seamen. The second boat was charged by the first mate, Samuel Hardy, and the third was controlled by the second officer, Mr. Parr. All were seasoned crew members who knew not only how to navigate, but also how to command these lifeboats. As captain, Josiah felt confident his men were in the best hands available.

With strong cord, Josiah lashed the two smaller boats to his longboat so all three could drift together. He wound the frayed rope through the oars of the boats and under the wooden slats as tightly as he could. This way they would have a greater chance of not capsizing in the roiling waves. Satisfied the boats were secure, Josiah encouraged the men to get some rest. That night, no one slept a wink. Instead, most of the crew remained transfixed by the scene of the burning vessel in front of them.

As *The Hornet* creaked into its final demise, the fire lit the kerosene and candles in the hull and at once started to shoot off flames. The sound was spectacular, creaking and splintering, then screaming, as if the sinking was a private Fourth of July firework display solely for the men.

By dawn, the ship yawned and sank into the black depths of the ocean, its hull still burning, a glowing eerie light emanating from its body.

A celebratory goodbye distracted the men for a few moments from the bitter truth: They were thousands of miles from the nearest land mass.

It could be months before harbor masters realized that *The Hornet* didn't arrive at its destination, as the ship was already far into its voyage, and the harbor master wouldn't send out distress signals. Even though Josiah had hoped for a ship to pass by before their boat disappeared, he understood that it was a futile wish. There was no way to alert anyone back on the mainland that the ship had sunk or that the crew had survived. Even if they knew, the options were limited. A search party would have few ideas of where to look or even what the last coordinates were. Their survival depended on the rescuers' ability to navigate the open ocean, like finding a needle in a haystack.

A few pieces of the doomed ship's wooden hull floated on the water's surface in front of them. Josiah could feel his crew's eyes rake over him as the awfulness of the situation was realized.

Drifting at Sea

On the eighth day adrift at sea, Josiah spotted two dolphins, their silvery fins slicing through the ocean, calling to each other with joyful clicks, defying the sea that had been so merciless to his men. He could feel his heart lift with a modicum of hope at the sight of the beautiful animals. Since *The Hornet* had sunk, the weather had been stormy, tossing the lifeboats and pelting them with rain squalls. The nights were pitch black—the men had brought no lanterns or torches, and the lack of light played with their ability to understand even where they were. They passed the nameless, rainy hours in fear, wondering if they were going to succumb to the dark, swirling ocean. There was nothing to do except think about food and stare out at the horizon.

The men started to look famished and despairing. Josiah was zapped of the resources he needed to encourage them. During the first days, he had given each man a small piece of salted pork, half a potato, and a piece of bread, but their food supplies were rapidly diminishing and he had to ration them to just half a biscuit a day each and small sips of water. He could tell the lack of food was getting to all of them. At first there was silence and despair. The men just looked out at the ocean, as if breaking the quietude would prevent them from reaching land. Downpours had been moving in and out; gray storm clouds would roll in, drench the men with rain, and then disappear. There was no time in between the squalls to dry off. Everyone was miserable and tempers were short.

When the weather finally began to cooperate, the sun became an even greater threat. Without the storms, the water had calmed, and the sun beat down on their heads all day long. The boats swirled in circles instead of moving across the waves, and there was no breeze to cool the men down. At night, cold rain lashed down with thunder and lightning. By morning, the men would be soaked to the bone, and by midafternoon, they were scorched by the sun. Their faces were burned red, and not even the heavy wool blankets could block out the strong rays or protect their vulnerable skin. The men cowered from the blistering heat.

While staring at the ocean one day, suddenly one of the mates shouted, "Look!" Everyone clambered to the side of the boat, following his pointed arm with their eyes. The man had seen a small, dark object rising and falling among the waves. What could it be? Another boat? As they approached the shape floating on the water, they discovered it was a small green sea turtle, fast asleep. They hushed their voices and hastily laid plans. One of the crew reached over, grabbed the turtle by the leg, and pulled it into the boat. The men were elated. Using their knives, they viciously hacked the animal to death.

Turtle meat was a delicacy, its flesh white and soft. The men feasted. After weeks of dried provisions and water, the protein gave a jolt of energy. Maybe they would reach land and survive after all.

Navigation to Nowhere

Josiah felt confident from studying his maps that they could reach the shores of Clarion Island, located off the coast of Mexico, on the way to the Sandwich Islands. He traced the proposed route using the compass and the maps he brought with him, his intuition guided by the sun's movement overhead. By his geographic calculations, they weren't very far.

"We are still alive and together," Josiah said. He stood at the front of the lifeboat and addressed the fatigued men. "We will reach Clarion Island. It is our only chance of survival."

In their faces he could see their disbelief.

He hoped his voice sounded strong enough, as the crew needed to follow him without question. Josiah knew mutiny could erupt at any moment, and he needed to keep his men calm. They all needed to share food, stay sharp, and not quarrel over how to divide the pickings among them.

The men's faces remained impassive. They didn't seem to respond one way or the other to the news of possible land. Josiah wasn't sure how to read the mindset of the disgruntled men. But his instincts told him that there was grumbling happening in the packed boats, especially the first mate's. Whispers had reached the captain's ear not only about a potential mutiny, but also about his possible demise. Henry Ferguson told him some of the crew were plotting to murder him. He started to sleep with his knife in his hand and kept it on him at all times.

On the eighteenth day at sea, Josiah decided to break the three ships apart. Almost ten days had passed since the turtle feast, and the boats hadn't come any closer to sighting land as Josiah had predicted. Day after day it had been just endless miles of sea. He thought they would soon see Clarion Island, but the weather took a turn for the worse. Rains and storm clouds came for another seven days, battering the men and shifting the boats further off course. Then, again, the sun would peak, beating down on them for hours, parching the men's lips and drying up every square inch of their skin, which had started to hang and wobble, resembling lizards' hides. The men were growing more despondent. They looked haggard, as if they had aged one hundred years in less than three weeks.

And then the wind died down and each day consisted of the three boats just bobbing on the water. The men weren't strong enough to row, and they were starting to lose their sanity from doing nothing. Something had to be done. Josiah reasoned that if they split the boats apart, they could pick up the wind more easily and move at greater speeds. If the boats remained lashed together, they would only have one chance at surviving. Separated, Josiah surmised, they had three chances. Each boat had a navigator, and they should be able to use their compasses and maps to sail their own course to land.

"My boat is still going to try to make it to Clarion Island," Josiah informed the men on the other vessels. "If you would like to follow us, you can. But it's your boat to run now, and I am sure you will make the judgment best seen fit."

By 11 a.m. that day, the boats separated from each other with the crew still on fairly good terms.

"We'll see you on the other side," the men promised each other.

There was some arguing about who would go on which boat, and in the end, Josiah's boat was once again left with fifteen men. They clamored into his boat after dividing what was left of the water and the meager food provisions. When, eventually, a gale separated the boats from each other, he wished the others godspeed, but inside thought, "We are all too weak to pull through, and unless we get a breeze soon, must all perish." They waved goodbye to the other lifeboats and drifted away.

On the twenty-first day at sea, as daylight rose after a night drenched in squalls and thunder, Josiah spotted a sail ahead. Hope leaped in his heart—were they going to be saved?

"Ahoy, sail ahead," he called out to his crew, jumping to his feet in excitement.

Many of the listless crew members were lying on the bottom of the boat, having spent the daylight hours too depleted to even raise their heads. It had been a long few days since they were separated from the other men. Surprisingly, they missed the companionship of the other two boats. They felt even more alone in the great ocean, completely convinced they would never make it out of its turbulent depths.

"Heave ho, men, let's pull," Josiah commanded, urging the famished, weak crew to grab the oars one last time and pull alongside the potential rescue ship. In unison they stroked the oars, pumping them, until they pulled up to the phantom ship and they realized that it was not salvation, but the first mate's boat they had left just days earlier. Bitter disappointment filled the boat, and Josiah could almost hear the crew laugh at his foolhardy quest, but he blocked the derision from his mind.

Josiah spoke jocularly with the first mate, asked him how the boat was doing, and divided some more food and water between the crew. They spoke for a short while, maybe twenty minutes, but time had become unmoored. Finally, they bid the other crew farewell and pushed off, swallowing their trepidation.

They never saw the other boats again.

Looking to Lady Luck

That afternoon, as if propelled by the brief interaction, Lady Luck smiled upon them. They caught a sea bird, splendid with its brown and white feathers rustling. The bird was as large as a duck, but the men soon found it didn't have much meat on its bones. It was almost like eating a pigeon. Regardless, the crew dined on their first fresh meat in weeks, sucking the delicate bones dry and licking the moisture off the feathers. Not one morsel of the bird was wasted, and it was accompanied by five small oysters, the size of a knuckle, to divide between them. Even though the oysters had dried out from being stuck in between the bird's feathers, they tasted refreshing. It had been a good day.

By May 29, Josiah reduced the ration to a quarter of a biscuit a day for each man. They had been on the open sea for more than three weeks with no rescue ship or land in sight. They had about a teacup left of water, some breadcrumbs, and a tin of ham left from *The Hornet*, but they mostly depended on what they could catch from the ocean. Gathering the strength to hunt the churning waters for sustenance was proving a problem. The men were giving up. They were scraping the leather from their boots and drinking the moisture that had been baked into the skin. They sucked the collars of their shirts, extracting moisture gathered from overnight dew. They licked the canvas that had previously held their butter and ham for any remaining salt or brine stuck on the material. There was still a large tin of tobacco on the boat, enough for each man to have a daily plug, and the moisture from the plant kept their mouths sated.

The men were too weak to stand, and if they leaned over the side of the boat they risked falling overboard, where they wouldn't be able to fight and would drown from the pull of the swirling ocean. Josiah could tell the men's minds were unquiet and he eventually uncovered another plot to murder him. The crew wanted to throw him overboard and steer the boat in another direction. Josiah had taken to sleeping with a hatchet under his hip, in case he was attacked. But he understood the men's resentment and anger. There was no sight of land, and Josiah had promised them they would have reached Clarion Island by now, but he couldn't admit defeat yet. Hope—along with food—was in meager supply.

At night, Josiah, without telling the crew, sought another route. Somehow they had overshot Clarion Island. Before he told the men, he needed an alternative.

"Men, let us be grateful God has granted us the opportunity to survive, but your concerns have encouraged me," said Josiah. "We will now set course and head straight for the Sandwich Islands."

Using the sun and his compass, Josiah estimated they were 1,000 miles from the Sandwich Islands. Everyone was very feeble, but Josiah knew it was their only hope. There was no other land mass within thousands of miles.

By Josiah's calculations it would take about three weeks to get there. It seemed God was on their side and the currents had been drifting them in the direction they needed to go, as if by divine intervention. He could only pray that the ships would eventually hit the Sandwich Islands.

The men had become resigned; there was no more talk of murders or mutiny, and during the day quiet descended over the boat. They were all reserving their strength. Sleeping all day had become normal. Josiah knew he had to do something to lift the men's spirits or they would all drift off into a slumber they would never wake up from.

"Crew, we are going to play a game," Josiah said to faint smiles from his men.

He came up with a sort of game, in which the men described delicious ten-course dinners to each other. The plan was to see who could entice the others the most. It didn't matter that the hunger pangs were gnawing at their ribs and their hearts—they knew they had no food to eat, so it seemed almost lighthearted to speak about the indulgence. The men meticulously planned the meals they were going to have once they reached the shore, each one topping the other with more extravagance. There'd be fowls cooked in sauce, chickens crisp with their skins on, ducks, and perfectly baked desserts, cookies, and tea. All the salivating talk awakened the men from their stupor.

At night they would dream of food and tell each other their thoughts when they woke. Most of the men didn't sleep more than two hours, forever jostled awake by the waves.

"I dream of such feasts and such feasts! Bread and fowl lining tables—and meat—everything smoking hot arranged on long tables," one of the crew, Seaman Cox, told the rapt group during his turn to explain to his mates what he dreamt of eating when they reached land. Cox continued to describe his thoughts: "And we reached across the table like ravenous wolves—and carried the dishes to our lips and ate and drank," he said. "And then we awoke and found the same starving comrades about us and the vacant sky and desolate sea."

The men listened to his tales, saddened by the ending, but to lighten the mood Josiah laughed and said, "I'll be happy just eating bread and butter every day of my life if we can get out of here."

Land at Last

By the twenty-eighth day, the remaining rations were a tea-spoonful of breadcrumbs and an ounce of ham, representing allocations so meager a kitten would die off their intake. The men couldn't even work up the strength to talk and there were no more conversations about feasts. They needed to conserve their energy. The next morning, the men woke to find that four small sardines had leapt into their boat. Joy filled the men's faces—at last there was some food. Using their knives, the crew quickly divided the tiny, bony fish between the fifteen men and ate them raw. It was only a nibble of food, but for the moment, the men pretended they were feasting.

The crew saved one of the sardines and presented it to Josiah. They wanted him to regain his strength and guide them to the Sandwich Islands. Their thoughts of mutiny were gone and they believed in their captain once more. Josiah refused to take it, saying he wanted the men to divide the fish equally and he would take only his share. The men refused to listen to him and insisted that he eat. After all, he was their captain and they needed him. Josiah obliged and ate the small sliver of fish. Tears would have run down his face if all the moisture in his body hadn't already dried.

On Monday, the thirty-eighth day after *The Hornet* had sunk, the third mate announced they were completely out of rations. Just the ham bone was left. They scraped the gristle off the bone and divided it among them. Afterward, they ripped off the tops of their boots and pounded the leather into a soft paste, and each man ate a small ration for dinner. Josiah broke apart the oak barrel the butter had been kept inside, and each man chewed on wooden pieces to suck out some of the grease that had been left behind. Splinters choked their mouths, but they pressed on, savoring any morsel of butter they were able to obtain.

Josiah could feel his strength quickly draining. He couldn't live much longer without nutrients. Some of the men were young and strong, but Josiah felt his age would not allow him to hold on much longer. With the last of his strength he wrote a letter to his wife and daughters, stating how much he loved them and that he would probably never see them again.

By early June there was no more food to eat. Josiah knew his men were starving to death. They were drinking three tablespoons of water a day—and nothing more. Josiah's head began to trouble him and he feared that he wouldn't live through another night. Still, Josiah encouraged the men to keep watch, as they had been doing since they boarded the boats so many fateful weeks earlier. One group of men rested, another scanned the horizon for any incoming boats or land, while the others scooped water out of the badly leaking boat. With constant tropical storms and trade winds dumping water into their boats, it became a daily task to keep them afloat.

On June 12, Josiah woke up, and he was still alive. It was his birthday and he wrote in his diary, "Thanking god for the opportunity for a new birthday for the soul, and work to be made clean for the kingdom of heaven." Neal Turner, one of the seamen, announced to everyone on the boat that he had given up. He laid down in the back and said he was going to die there. It didn't look like Neal would make it through the night. Some of the men didn't move to save him. They wanted him to die.

Although Josiah had never heard any of them discuss cannibalism, he knew if Neal didn't survive, the men would surely eat their comrade.

Samuel Ferguson was also very sick. His tongue had turned black and was stuck to the roof of his mouth. In the morning, his brother Henry fed him his ration of brackish water. It was just one sip.

There was one more day of water left, and there was no way the men would survive once that ran out. Josiah couldn't even find the will to write in his journal to note the date or anything more about their conditions.

On, Friday, June 15, day forty-three, Josiah thought he saw a glimmer of land ahead. He didn't dare say anything to the other men in case it was a false alarm. There had been many previous sightings in which the men had thought they had seen land, only to be bitterly disappointed, so Josiah held his tongue. But by 10:30 a.m., Josiah was sure the emerald coast of the Sandwich Islands lay before them as gem-like and precious as the men had imagined. They had traveled over 4,000 miles without spotting land, and then, suddenly, there it was.

"God be forever praised for his infinite mercy to us!" shouted Henry as the survival dawned on them.

It took six hours to navigate the boat around the volcanic rocks before they were able to hit land. Only Josiah and a few of the other able-bodied men could assist, as most of the crew was too ill to row the oars. The men were met on the shore at Laupahoehoe by the Kanakas, the Pacific Islanders living on the Sandwich Islands at the time. They took one look at the famished seamen lying on the bottom of the boat and carried them up the hills to safety.

All fifteen men on Josiah's ship survived *The Hornet* wreck and forty-three days on the open sea. The men from the other two boats were never seen again. Samuel Clements, known as Mark Twain, reported his first huge newspaper story on the shipwreck, which catapulted him to future fame. Six weeks later, Josiah set back to New York via steamship and spent the remainder of his life commanding vessels across the oceans.

Dina Mironovna Pronicheva
Ravine of Death
Kiev, Ukraine, 1941

There was a noise, a slight banging of something hard onto the ground, then a low murmur in German. The hot breath of the soldier's words came so close to Dina that it felt like they were being whispered directly into her ear. She tried not to whimper, biting her tongue so hard she could feel the bitter taste of blood in her mouth. The liquid trickled down her throat.

"Demydenko, come here, fill it in," the soldier commanded. Sounds of metal scraping and a soft rustle pervaded the chilly nighttime air as the soldiers started to shovel mounds of sand into the open mass graves. Dina was lying face-up, sandwiched between piles of corpses, the beaten, bloodied bodies she'd heard die. Small, hard grains of sand clogged her ears, her nostrils, and her eyes. She couldn't breathe. There was not enough air. Her throat constricted. She could feel herself start to suffocate.

"No, Dina Pronicheva, you are not going to die here," she told herself, "not after what you have made it through today." She'd rather die at the hands of German soldiers than be buried alive, she decided, flailing against the shifting grains of sand. Slowly, she unstuck her good right hand from underneath her damaged side. Her left arm was bloodied and crushed, its sharp white bones sticking through her shirt after the soldier had stomped on her body earlier. She tried not to look at her arm or remember the deadening weight of the black boots upon her back, so heavy she'd felt and heard the clink of steel wedged inside his heel.

If Dina saw what had actually happened to her, she knew she wouldn't be able to move forward. Gathering her strength, she lifted her good arm and wiped the fine sand coating the corners of her dry mouth. Air rushed into her lungs, and she started to cough. Loudly. She stopped herself, breathing the debris back into her lungs. She couldn't let the soldiers hear a single sound. They would shoot her on sight. And she wanted to live.

Massacre in Kiev

At 7 o'clock that morning, Dina had left her house to head to her mother's, leaving the sweet forms of her toddler children still cuddled under their feather blankets. She left her husband, Viktor, and mother-in-law to mind the children. It was safer that way. After all, they were Russian Jews. Even though, through marriage, she had a resident card stating she was Ukrainian, she knew her curly brown hair and flashing dark eyes were a dead giveaway.

It had been less than twenty-four hours since the order appeared pasted throughout the streets of Ukraine's capital, Kiev. They read: "All Jews are to take warm and valuable things and appear at eight in the morning on September 29 at Degtyarev Street. The punishment for failing to appear is execution." The signature was from the commandant's office.

Rumors had fervently spread that soldiers were going to purge the city of Jews. They didn't know where they were going to be sent. Dina's parents, Miron and Ana, thought they were bound for Soviet territory. With her two brothers gone to the front with the Red Army, Dina was going to accompany her parents and younger sister to the destination that was indicated on the sign. She was going to explain to the people in charge that it was a mistake to deport her family. She needed to be brave; after all, when she'd decided to marry Viktor, a non-Jew, they had supported her decision.

Dina searched for their faces in the growing crowd.

The familiar cobblestone streets were crowded. Families she had known for years were milling around, tattered ragbags enclosed with valuables clenched in their hands. Others had satchels tied to their backs, their edges bulging. Cars and two-wheeled carts piled with goods clogged the streets. People were walking around confused, and everyone had the same vacant look in their eyes, as if they didn't know what lay ahead. Mothers held infants; elderly people struggled on their canes. Dina could see the sparkle of gold spill from the luggage of a family struggling with their belongings. It seemed they had taken everything. She could even see dishes peeking out from the top of their bags. Where did they think they were going? A sense of foreboding filled her chest. This wasn't what she had pictured. Something wasn't right.

Sucking in her breath, Dina clutched for the phantom chubby toddler hands of her children. There was nothing to hold onto but empty space. She prayed that the soldiers would let her return home by the afternoon.

A horde had formed, and as it moved slowly toward the intersection of Melnyk Street, Dina thought nearly every Jew in Kiev was gathered outside. Fortunately, it wasn't winter yet, and the weather was still relatively mild. In front of her, near the black iron gates of the Jewish cemetery, Dina could see some sort of roadblock had been put into place.

In the center of the cement blocks was a hole that looked to be an entrance. Above the roadblock, barbed wire was threaded through the cement blocks. Guarding the entrance were drab Russian tanks lined up in a row, their heavy armed guns pointed in the direction of the crowd. Dina realized the guards were in German uniforms. They were wearing helmets, with identification numbers on their breasts and rifles by their sides. These were different soldiers mixed in with the Ukrainian ones, easily identifiable by their black uniforms with gray cuffs.

Dina watched as her fellow Jews filed through the makeshift entrance in a single column. Herding them forward was a tall, striking man with a long, black, Cossack mustache. Dina heard the Jews call him "Mr. Shevchenko," like the Ukrainian poet. He was wearing a heavily embroidered shirt, and in their language he cajoled the walkers, and his mannerisms spoke of death.

Fear filled Dina's throat, but there was no way to turn back. Soldiers holding guns lined the street every few feet. Behind her, a walled mass of people slowly pushed her forward, and ahead, her elderly parents and sister entered the queue. Her heart leaped at the sight of their familiar faces. Her parents looked so defeated and dulled. Their winter jackets were wrapped around them tightly, but her beloved younger sister was a bright spot. Her long brown hair curled around her shoulders. She turned and spoke sharply to their parents, and they followed her obediently. Dina wanted to rush over to her family and pull them out of the line. But something stopped her from threading herself through the crowd to reach them. Dina stayed where she was in the pack, said nothing, and kept walking just like everyone else. At that moment, she hated herself. She passed through the entrance.

Gates of Death

Behind the cemetery gates was an intense mass of confusion. It was utter chaos. German soldiers were selecting people, roughly pushing some to the left and others to the right. If they protested, the soldiers used the butts of their guns to draw blood. Dina could see her parents go straight while she was sent to the right. As soon as she made her way out of the clogged entrance, a German soldier came up to her and roughly took off the fur coat she was wearing. She didn't protest, as his eyes were cold and aggressive. Dina struggled as the biting cold entered her thin silk shirt. She shivered.

Another enormous soldier with bulging muscles wearing a tight uniform came up to her and whispered into her ear, "Come and sleep with me, and I'll let you out."

Dina looked at him with disdain, as if he were out of his mind. At her dismissal, he skulked away. She was used to men propositioning her. An actress in the Kiev theater, she was celebrated, and had often been approached by admirers. The soldier turned back into the crowd. As soon as he left, she considered chasing after him in an effort to save herself. Why didn't she take the opportunity? But the soldier had already disappeared into the disordered crowd.

The group she was huddled with started to walk, herd-like, unsure of where they were going. They just kept walking forward. Again, Dina thought maybe she should have taken the soldier's offer; it would have been better than wandering around here, without knowing what was going to happen to her.

Suddenly Dina heard the voice of an old man in the crowd behind her, "My children, help me walk. I'm blind."

Dina felt sorry for the old man and went to help him. He had a long white beard, was wearing a tattered black jacket, and walked bent forward, using a wooden cane. His eyes were closed shut by illness. He seemed to be a very religious and pious man. She perceived an aura radiating from him as the others fell away.

She took his cold hand in her thin palm and asked, using terms of honor appropriate for an elderly man, "Granddad, where are we being taken?"

"Don't you know, child? We're going to pay God the last honors," he replied.

Ahead of her, Dina could see two rows of German soldiers lined up shoulder to shoulder, forming a dense barrier. No one could pass through their linked bodies. They were bearing big sticks, rubber truncheons, and vicious dogs, foaming at the mouth. As the people in front of her passed through the corridor, the soldiers set upon them horribly, beating them with the sticks and the truncheons. Screams filled the air. A man caught in the horrific beatings tried to run away and, in a flash, the dogs were set upon him, their snarling teeth white against their shiny black coats. They bit into his flesh and clothes, tearing off chunks of his bloodied skin as he screamed in horror.

Dina watched, frozen. The slaughter continued all around her. The soldiers beat the Jews terribly with whatever they had; they used their hands, or their steel-toed boots. Some policemen were wearing knuckledusters—strips of brass rings—across their hands. One punch against the metal ripped a man's skin down to the bone. And there was no discrimination. Soldiers were hitting women and children as they passed. As the soldiers beat the incoming Jews, forcing them to strip their clothes, rivulets of blood ran down their pale bodies. Women screamed in shame and tried to cover their private parts with their hands. It was a futile effort. The soldiers laughed, their blatant cruelty astounding. Dina couldn't believe her eyes—their world had been turned upside down.

As a Jew growing up in the Ukraine, Dina had witnessed wanton brutality before. She'd seen pogroms, when authorities dispelled Jews from their houses and beat them into submission. But she had never seen anything like this. She wanted to shield her eyes with her hands but at the same time appear brave.

Dina looked around at the unfolding chaos. She was frightened. Underneath her dress her knees and elbows were shaking with unfettered abandon. She couldn't control the urge to flee. How was she going to get out of here? She turned back, making her way through the crowd, who had yet to see what lay ahead of them. Images of the naked, writhing bodies ran through her head. She desperately wanted to get home to her husband and children. It was a mistake to go there in the first place. She should be allowed to leave. She was married to a Russian man! She was a respected actress. Her mother-in-law was a pious Russian Orthodox observer with religious icons hanging all around her apartment. Her children were probably eating beets and beans at their scarred wooden kitchen table right now.

As she walked and fumed, Dina understood there was nowhere to go. Even if she was married to a Russian man, she was registered with the government as a Jew. The authorities would come find her; there was no way to escape. It was better to go die with her parents. She turned back and walked silently toward the corridor where the German soldiers were waiting. Shortly before she reached the front of the line, she heard a voice cry out. It was a voice from her childhood.

"Darling, you don't look like a Jew! Escape!" It was her mother, screaming. Dina heard her plea and sought out her face in the crowd.

It took a moment to pinpoint where the voice was coming from, but then she spotted her beloved parents naked, bloodied, and shivering. She wanted to rush to protect them, but self-preservation told her she couldn't. In front of them was the body of her much-loved younger sister. She was naked, lying on the ground, and a German policeman was savagely beating her, kicking her head, face, and body while she screamed in pain. Dina's parents watched, their faces contorted. Dina couldn't bear to look. She turned away without saying a word. Shame flooded every molecule of her body.

Dina squared her shoulders and walked straight ahead without stopping. This was the second time she had to abandon her family. She knew the only way through was to press forward, so she passed under the soldier's blows raining down on her back and shoulders, the baton's hard wood breaking against her delicate skin. She could feel every strike, but she walked upright and endured it.

On the other side, she went straight up to a policeman and immediately asked him in Ukrainian where the commandant was. He asked why she wanted the commandant, and Dina answered, her head tilted proudly, "I am a Ukrainian, not a Jew. I had come to accompany my coworkers and have ended up here by accident."

She hoped in that moment he believed her story. He gave Dina a strange look and asked for her papers. She showed him her trade-union membership card and work book, where nationality is not indicated. The soldier reviewed the worn documents. He believed Dina because her surname was Russian. He pointed to a mound where a small group of people were sitting and said, "Sit down and wait until evening. We'll let you go after we've shot all the Jews."

Dina took a seat on the sandy mound, crossed her arms, and waited. She couldn't move, taking in the horrors of the scene unfolding in front of her. People were continuing to be stripped naked and beaten senseless. One man was laughing hysterically as he lay near death, pools of blood near his head. He was obviously losing his mind in the seconds before his demise. People were walking all over the bodies lying on the ground, as if the minute they fell, they ceased to exist.

Babies were being torn from their mothers and thrown over the narrow sandy walls into pits the soldiers had dug, and the women screamed in horror at the squeals of their children. But Dina could do nothing. She sat there quietly. If she was going to survive for her children, she had to convince the guards she was Russian so they would let her go. She was positive there was no other way.

As she waited, soldiers started to lead groups of two to three people through the sandy area, and she never saw them return.

Evening crept over the landscape and cold air rushed in. Before darkness fell, a black sedan pulled up, and a German soldier exited the passenger door.

"All the Jews need to be shot," Dina overhead him briskly tell the Ukrainian officers. "If we leave one of them alive, they will tell everyone what they have seen here today. That can't happen."

Ravine of Death

The soldiers led all the remaining Jews over to the sandy wall. There was no crying, fighting, or attempting to run away. It was as if they understood they were being led to their death, but realized they were powerless to stop the onslaught. Even though the soldiers had said they were going to let her go, Dina knew she was going to end up in one of those groups. She looked to run, but everywhere she turned there were soldiers. There was nowhere to go, so when she was nudged off the mound, she got up and followed orders.

The soldiers led her group of ten down the ravine wall to a ledge. No one spoke, and they didn't try and run or fight. They just followed. She could tell the soldiers were tired. On the other side of the quarry, Dina could make out the shadows of more soldiers. They were sitting on tree stumps in front of a crackling bonfire, the flames leaping in the night, as though they were camping and getting ready to make coffee. Sounds of their high-pitched laughter trailed through the air.

Dina didn't look at anyone in her group. There were groups of people huddled in front of her waiting their turn to die. Behind her she could feel warm bodies pressing up against her as they all waited.

The soldiers lined up the first group against a ledge, took out their machine guns, and sprayed them with bullets. Blood splattered into the air as their screams were halted. All the people fell backward into the deep abyss behind them. Dina clenched her fists and squeezed her eyes shut; her group was next in line. In addition to the sandy pits dug all along the area, there was a deep, wide pit obviously built for the killing. Cut along a jagged edge, the ledge was difficult to traverse, and all the blood and tears made the shelf slippery to stand on. Using their long guns and bayonets, the soldiers prodded her group toward the precipice. Dina could see mounds of dead and bloodied bodies below in the deep pit constructed for mass murder.

She had only a moment to make a split-second decision.

In the instant the gunshots rang out, Dina threw herself hard onto the solid ground. Her face met with the edge of a rock that pulverized the side of her cheek. She could feel her thin skin tear open, but she felt no pain. As she rolled backward into the ravine, on top of the sharp bony bodies below all she felt was the will to live.

Slowly, the world started coming back into focus. A starry, nighttime sky twinkled overhead, oblivious to the suffering below. Above her she could hear the clinking and clacking of what sounded like silverware and plates. The soldiers were eating dinner. And then Dina heard the moans. The otherworldly sounds of pain rose into the air. There was weeping and hiccups. She could hear the soft prayers of mothers as they lay next to their children, comforting them for the great unknown. Their last unselfish act as a parent.

Dina felt the side of her face. It was covered in warm blood. The bones on the right side of her head were tender to the touch. Cracks of bone poked through the skin. She dropped her hand and she didn't move any further, letting the thick, red liquid fill her nose and eyes. Torchlights were circulating over the fallen bodies, and Dina could see German soldiers checking the corpses. The soldiers pulled out a shotgun and fired point blank at anyone who moved an inch. Someone groaned loudly next to Dina and the soldiers edged closer. She stayed as still as she could and closed her eyes tightly, hoping her bloodied body and cracked face would convince them she was dead.

A moment later, a shot rang out and the person next to her was silenced by a bullet in the chest. Maybe she jumped. Maybe she didn't. But then a German soldier grabbed her and turned her over. Her clothes had not been pierced by any bullets. The soldier called his compatriot over to take a look. Together they lifted her up and struck her across the head, but Dina did not make a sound. She stayed as still as stone. One of the soldiers put his foot on her chest. He pulled back her hand, and pushing on her breastbone with his weighted boot, sent shooting pains through her body. But she didn't react. The soldiers decided she was dead and moved on to check other bodies. Their footsteps faded away in the darkness.

Dina let out a breath. She was still alive. Then she heard a distinct muffled sound. The soldiers were back. There was a scraping noise, and she could hear hard metal hit against the ground. Mounds of sand were being shoveled over her face, sticking to the congealed blood. She could feel herself starting to suffocate and used small bursts of air from her nose to push away the grit. Dirt started to cover her eyes. She kept them closed and resisted the urge to wipe the debris away. It grew dark and then everything was quiet. After Dina became accustomed to the gloom, she lifted her arms from her sides and used her hands to claw away the thin layer of sand that had been poured over her body. The soldiers didn't do a very good job of burying the dead. She wiped the sand from her eyes as best as she could and glanced around to evaluate her predicament. She could make out the shapes of four giant walls around her, including the wall she had plummeted from. With quiet desperation, she started to crawl toward the lowest point of the entrance.

Dina remembered coming into the pit that way, so there must be a way to get back out. As she moved past the bloodied corpses, she heard a voice whisper, "Help."

Dina saw a skinny, teenaged boy. He was gaunt and dressed in a thin top and high cloth trousers. He wasn't wearing a jacket. His dark hair was tinged with blood along his forehead, but otherwise he looked unharmed.

In a whisper, he introduced himself to Dina.

"I'm Motia," he said. Dina motioned for him to follow her, to crawl as silently as possible.

They made their way over the dead bodies to the sandy walls of the ravine. As they tried to scale their way up the side, there was nothing for them to grasp and they kept sliding back down. Covered in sand and frustration, their feet were slimy with the blood of the bodies they were stepping on. Finally, they were able to gain a toehold using one of the tree roots that snaked into the ravine, and lifted themselves out onto higher ground.

Dawn was breaking, and the pearl-gray sky was streaked a beautiful pink. But daylight meant trouble. They were exposed, and the soldiers would be able to see that they were alive. Dina knew they needed to hide immediately or risk being discovered. Dina hissed at Motia to climb behind some thick green bushes that hedged the outskirts of the ravine. They stayed there silently as they heard the familiar sound of German soldiers plodding in their direction.

The soldiers stopped nearby, continuing to bury the corpses. Dina spied them shoveling sand and dirt over the bodies, hiding any evidence of the massacre. For hours she and Motia didn't dare move. She didn't even swallow, not wanting to waste the saliva in her throat or make a sound. Dina began to hallucinate, and saw her father, mother, and sister in front of her wearing long white robes and turning somersaults. Dina reached out to try and grab them, but as she clenched her fists they were empty, and she realized it was just an illusion. Bereft, Dina lost consciousness and collapsed.

A Chance to Escape

When she regained consciousness, Motia was sitting beside her crying. He thought she had died. Nighttime had fallen again and darkness gave them cover to crawl across a large meadow to a copse of trees nearby. Dina thought it would be a good place for them to hide and would provide a safe shelter.

Motia agreed to go first as he was smaller. Hugging the ground, he inched ahead, Dina on his heels, when a shot rang out. Motia collapsed into the mud. Dina could see blood trickling from his broken skull where the bullet had hit. She stopped herself from screaming and rolled back into the ravine, praying the soldiers didn't come over.

She waited until darkness was at its peak and then crawled back to the meadow where Motia's body lay. She did the best to cover his small frame by scraping some of the gritty sand over his body. It was futile, as the ground was too hard. There would be no proper burial for Motia. As she rested her trembling, dirt-stained fingers, she cried over his small corpse, as if he were her own son.

Dina had made it through the night. She was still alive. But she had to make it out of the ravine. She scanned her surroundings and to her left discovered what seemed like a pathway to escape. Shakily, she crawled to her feet and scrambled toward the path. Dina soon realized she was standing in the middle of a garbage dump. Refuse was piled everywhere.

By her feet, she spotted two round, green tomatoes. They were untouched, with a little damage on the sides. It had been two days since she had eaten so her stomach rumbled with hunger. But she didn't have a moment to spare, as she needed to hide first, so she left the valuable food untouched.

Dina covered herself with piles of garbage, rags, and leaves, and placed a discarded woven basket over her head. Completely hidden, she shut her eyes for some much needed rest. By the time she awoke, the day had already passed and it was nighttime again. Dina shook off the refuse and knew she couldn't survive this way for much longer. She could feel how weak and tired she was getting after the stress and not eating for the past few days, and she could hardly move one foot in front of another. She needed to escape.

Dina decided to crawl toward the trees she and Motia had seen. It took her almost the entire night, but suddenly she was in the forest. She could see a house and a shed with a low light burning in the window.

Maybe the residents of the house would help Dina. She stood up and made her way toward the open shed, when a mangy dog jumped out and started barking loudly. Dina stepped back in fear. She tried to quiet the dog's frenzied yelping, but he wouldn't stop.

"How did you get here?" Dina heard a women's voice ask. A Ukrainian farmer woman with a handkerchief tied under her chin appeared.

"I'm coming back from the trenches. I'm from Bila Tserkva, and asked about the way to the city commandant, who could help me get home," Dina could see fear in the women's eyes, so she carefully answered.

"We'll be able to show you the way," the farmer woman answered, and called out for her son. He appeared, and the woman barked an order at him. He ran off into the woods while Dina waited with the woman. The son returned later with a German soldier.

He pointed at Dina and said, "See, a Jew, Sir."

The soldier walked up to Dina and slapped her across the face. She touched the red mark on her cheek. "Follow me," he yelled. Dina followed him into the house, where there were other Germans sitting around the table eating breakfast. Dina could feel bile rise in her throat. She hadn't eaten for four days, but she didn't want any food. She couldn't sit with these murderers. She shook her head, denying herself the meal.

The soldier ordered the other residents to guard her, and then left. As soon as he was gone, they got up and made Dina clean the table, kitchen, and windows. Bent with exhaustion, she didn't resist. As best as she could, she used wet cloths to wipe away the gathered grime.

When the soldier returned, he motioned for Dina to follow him. He was with two other girls who appeared to be around 16 or 17 years old. They were dressed in simple clothes. Together they walked outside and Dina recognized it was the same place where the soldiers had forced everyone to take off their clothes earlier. She had spent days crawling from that ravine and those horrible memories only to end up in the same spot. There were piles of clothes and shoes everywhere. Sitting by the discarded items were a woman, her baby, and a nurse. The infant was screaming loudly, and the nurse was trying to calm her.

The nurse took pity on Dina, who was trembling and streaked with blood. She spread out her overcoat on the floor and indicated to Dina that she should sit down, drawing the woolly fabric over Dina's bare legs.

"My name is Liuba," she said.

Dina was overcome by the generosity of the stranger, but she held her tears. She sat there calmly until evening, when a large truck filled with prisoners of war pulled up.

Dina and the other girls were told to climb onto the open-sided lorry with benches lining the back. Dina and Liuba made a pact to jump off the truck if they found they were going to be taken to be slaughtered. Dina would rather die fighting. After a few minutes, the truck pulled into a garage across from the Jewish cemetery. The garages were full, so after a brief stop, the truck pulled away.

There was confusion about where they were headed. There was screaming, and some of the passengers were banging on the window. Dina saw this as her chance to escape. If she could make it out of the ravine, she could run away from the soldiers. She could make it home and find her children and her husband. Thoughts of seeing them fueled her determination. She would survive the war. Dina clenched her fists, nodded to Liuba, and with her last bit of strength, she counted: one, two, three.

Dina jumped over the side of the truck. By the time she heard Liuba's feet hit the ground, she was already running, fast and free into the night.

Dina Mironovna Pronicheva is one of the few known survivors of the Babi Yar massacre in Ukraine, which killed 33,000 Jews. Dina ended up surviving the war as did her two children, Vladimir and Lidia, who spent most of the fighting living in orphanages. Dina searched for her children and found them in March 1944. Her husband, Viktor, did not survive. He was arrested and shot for unknown reasons. The rest of her immediate family perished at Babi Yar. It is not known if Liuba survived the massacre. Dina spent the remainder of her life working as an actress in the Ukraine. She testified about her experiences during war crime trials in Kiev.

Ada Blackjack
Arctic Expedition
Wrangel Island, 1921–1923

For Christmas dinner, Ada Blackjack made some salted seal meat, hard bread, and tea to eat with the crew of the Stefansson Expedition. She set out plates and silverware for herself and the four other members of her team. There had not been much to celebrate over the past few months as they battled the desolate Arctic winter, starving and isolated.

It was 1922, almost a year since she had left her home and been separated from her young son, Bennett. But Ada didn't complain. She knew something of the hard life. She had been separated from her abusive husband and was barely scraping by when, in the fall of 1921, she was made an offer she couldn't refuse. The ship's captain offered Ada, a seamstress, $1,200 to join their exploratory unit to Wrangel Island, an archipelago in the Arctic Ocean not far off the coast of Alaska, close to Russia. They needed someone to care for the men, cook, clean, and sew and repair their clothes and equipment. As an Iñupiat Inuit, she understood the harsh realities germane to the area, and could help the team of young crewmen navigate this difficult terrain.

Ada didn't readily agree to go on the voyage. Concerns colored her hesitation, as she could tell the crew were inexperienced. Still, the leader of the party, Vilhjalmur Stefansson, a Canadian who spent years mapping the Arctic and sought to claim Wrangel Island, was very persuasive. He told the crew and Ada a compelling story, one of glory for their country and an abundance of riches for their families. Plus, "Fame," Stefansson whispered into their ears, and Ada could feel the tide shift against her better judgment.

Nome, Alaska, where Ada was born and raised, was a small village hugging the Bering Sea, and authorities applied pressure when it was necessary. Locals wanted Ada to join the voyage so she could make some funds to support her child.

When the sheriff knocked on the door of her house, Ada understood turning down the captain's offer wasn't going to be an option. All of Nome knew she was down on her luck and didn't have enough money to properly take care of her child. The sheriff spoke in a threatening manner, telling her the money from the expedition could last years. Not taking it was a foolish choice that the sheriff didn't recommend. He reasoned that Ada could finally get on her feet and provide for her child as she dreamed. Reluctantly, Ada agreed.

Before Ada left Nome, she purchased sinew, needles, a thimble, and some linen thread, hoping the supplies would be enough to last for the entire journey. She left her son in the care of her sister, Rita, and boarded the vessel *Silver Wave*, commanded by Captain Jack Hammer, who had spent many years navigating the complex Arctic waters. From the onset, Ada had had a bad feeling. She didn't know how the ship was going to nose its way through the ice-clogged water. There were floes everywhere, and a less-experienced captain would certainly bring down the ship.

Remote Island

When the boat landed at Wrangel Island, Ada's first thought was that they should turn back, as the island was so remote. It took weeks to sail there and was smack in the middle of the Arctic Ocean, 100 miles from the Siberian coast with seemingly no other landmarks or islands nearby. But, instead, she squared her shoulders and disembarked. She had made a promise, and she was going to keep it.

The island was bigger than she expected. Miles stretched in front of her, a flat plateau of wild grasses on which majestic animals roamed. There were musk oxen, with their shaggy brown coats sweeping the ground and their gnarled horns ripping the grasses; arctic foxes with their luxurious white fur and sniffing black snouts; and playful walruses gathered upon rock foundations surrounding the island. The explorers were ecstatic. They were claiming a piece of paradise for Canada. Ada kept quiet. She knew these lands were harsh and uninhabitable for good reason.

But the expedition was not going as planned. When they had arrived at Wrangel Island, it seemed as if the promises made by the captain prior to the expedition were going to come true. The lands were abundant and the animals traipsed the terrain undisturbed. For the first few months the explorers trapped foxes, geese, ducks, seals, and even polar bears and walruses, but it seemed the animals had since disappeared. It had been ages since they had fresh meat. The ice had frozen the sea surrounding the islands, so no boats could get in or out. The reinforcements they were expecting never came, and the crew wasn't experienced enough to hunt in the cold. They didn't know how to trap animals in the blinding snow or pinpoint the targets enough for a clean shot. Ammunition ran out, with no food to show for their valiant efforts.

Ada hung back. She had learned from her husband how men hated to be challenged, especially by a woman. Every time she spoke out of turn, he had beaten her senseless. While she knew how to hunt and trap, she didn't want to hurt the explorers' efforts. They were so confident in their skills. As the only woman there, she didn't want their anger directed at her. She had no way to defend herself, so Ada kept away. She cooked the meager meals with the supplies they had remaining and darned their clothes.

Hope, which had been so abundant, quickly faded. They wished a ship would arrive soon with food and more assistance, but as the days passed it became clear help may not soon arrive. So the men decided they needed to bring in reinforcements or leave the island. If they stayed, they would surely all perish.

The team assigned to stay on the island—Lorne Knight, Allan Crawford, Fred Maurer, and Milton Galle—decided to trek to Siberia to search for supplies or villages that could assist their expedition. The plan was to walk 700 miles across the frozen Chukchi Sea between Alaska and Russia. They had spent the last few weeks hauling wood to the camp to light fires for warmth, and cooking and preparing everything for while they were away. Over their Christmas dinner that year, they planned their upcoming expedition, the bonfire lighting their lean faces. Excitement permeated the air. They were going to finally take matters into their own hands and stop waiting for reinforcements. They were going to do something.

"I'll sew you boys some skins to wear on your trip," Ada interjected quietly into their conversation. She was glad there was anticipation in the air, as lately the mood at the camp had been so downcast. She had just wondered if she would live to the next Christmas.

On January 8, the men set out, Ada waving them off from the camp. Although she was afraid to be left alone, she had faith in her ability to survive. Just two weeks later, Ada looked up from her sewing to see the explorers straggling back. This time they were dragging a makeshift sled, and Knight was strapped into it. During the trip Knight had become very sick and they felt they had to return to the camp. He was feverish and very weak, but still he encouraged the others to continue their expedition. Knight and Ada would stay behind as the remaining three explorers went out again for help.

Counting the Days

Before Crawford, Maurer, and Galle set off, they promised they would return with a boat. However, they said, if the waters were frozen, they would come back for the remaining crew with a dog sled. Either way they would be back, Galle said. When they left, they took a team of five dogs and a big sled of supplies with them. Little was left behind.

Once they were gone, the camp was quiet, with Knight lying on his cot most of the day and Ada caring for him. A week later Knight seemed to be feeling better, and he tried to help by chopping wood and bringing it to the sleep tent. Ada monitored him carefully. She didn't want him to overexert himself. His eyes were still red-rimmed with fever, and he had yet to regain his strength.

"Maybe it is better to stay in bed," she told him, but Knight looked at her with such anger, as if she was disrespecting him, so she bit her tongue. Minutes later, he collapsed onto the ground. His eyes could barely open and his breathing was extremely shallow. Ada checked his pulse and knew she needed to get him to his cot. But Knight was a big ox of a man and she was slight, standing at just over five feet tall with an open, round face and dark almond eyes that were barely visible peeping out from behind the white fox fur of her parka. But Ada was determined and stronger than she looked. She dragged back Knight into the tent and poured some cold water on his face, shocking him awake.

"I'll chop the wood and get the water, Mr. Knight," she said. "I've done this type of work down home." He closed his eyes and nodded, his pride defeated. Ada needed to take control if they were going to survive.

Every day, Ada went out to set the animal traps, but they were bare. She rationed the meat from their rapidly dwindling preserved supply and judged that they only had a few days left of provisions. Knight was conscious but too weak to get out of bed yet.

Occasionally Knight would share his Bible with Ada. She loved to trace the dense words with her finger, as she had never owned a book before, although she learned to read and write at missionary school when she was living in Nome. Mouthing the words, Ada practiced her reading and deflected any conversation with Knight. She didn't want him to know about their dire food situation and become discouraged. She thought she still had time to figure something out.

And then, days later, there was a white fox with a full coat of fur caught in one of the traps. Ada had never eaten fox before. In her village they used the fur for their clothes, and she had sewn many as trim onto parkas, but the meat went to the dogs. In her culture, it was bad luck to imbibe their spirits.

But now, there was no choice—they needed to eat it for their survival. That night, she cooked the meat on the fire and, for the first time in two months, they ate fresh food. The next day, she felt fine and had conquered her own superstitions, but all her uncertainties came rushing back when she felt queasy in her stomach a few days later. The next day she went out to check the traps again, and before she left, Knight handed her the Bible and let her touch its worn leather cover and run her fingers over the cracked pages for luck.

"You can have it," he said to Ada. She looked at him in shock. Nobody had ever given her anything before. Shyly, she nodded her head. The Bible must have brought her good luck, for in one of the traps there was a large male fox—a fat one. One day melted into the next as they waited for the expedition crew to return, and every day Ada continued setting the traps for foxes, skinning and eating her catches. She used their fur to make clothes and add to their warm supplies. She started to craft a belt out of the fine, dark black tails to pass the time.

Ada was lonely, as Knight could barely talk. Occasionally he would muster some energy, but most of the time he slept. His legs were getting stronger. They were skinny, but the blue spots that covered them were healed. It had been nearly two months since the other expedition team members left, and Ada began considering that they may never return.

Snow still blanketed the ground, and hard ice crunched underfoot, but spring was on its way. Ada's health was deteriorating; she got every ailment possible. Her tooth ached, her eyes swelled, her throat hurt. She was in so much pain that she wrote in her diary that if her body was found, all her belongings should go to her son, Bennett. She didn't have much—just what was stuffed in her rucksack—but she wanted her young son to have the black fox belt Ada had worked so hard on.

That night was tough, and she wasn't sure she would live until the morning. But when she opened her eyes the next day, she was still alive and felt marginally better. Ada celebrated by opening a canister of tea and biscuits from their hard tack supplies. The wind had been blowing hard, with snow drifts racking one side of the camps, so she appreciated the warm liquid. She blew hard on her chapped hands before she set off once again for the traps.

It was so bleak out. Ada counted the days; it was the beginning of April. She had been at the camp with Knight for almost three months, and still, there was no sign of the others returning. Little life surrounded them. Ada trudged through the snow drifts to check the traps and found a frozen fox inside one, but it was nothing but skin and bones so she didn't even bother bringing it back to the camp. That night she opened a can of cold oil to drink and finished a pair of yarn gloves for Galle in case he ever returned.

From Hope to Despair

By mid-April the sun started to shine, and Ada started to feel hopeful. Maybe the snow would thaw quickly and the crew would return to rescue them. They would all sail back to the mainland, never to see Wrangel Island again. The thought kept Ada satiated as she began her daily routine, and then she returned to the camp to check on Knight, who'd started complaining of his swollen leg. When Ada arrived he was lying on the cot, his face strained. "My head," he whispered, and refused the tea she offered. Ada used all their good provisions on Knight, trying to make him comfortable, but could do nothing about his refusals. Ada ducked out for some fresh air and spotted a storm cloud brewing in the distance. More snow was coming. Her heart fell and despair soured her mind. How was she going to make it through the days?

Knight was growing weaker, and as the shadow of death approached, he grew mean. Every day he would say something horrible to Ada. She tried her best to ignore him, but he attacked her at her lowest points. When she stopped in that morning to build the fire, Knight hissed at her, "Blackjack was a good man. He was right in everything and you deserved to be treated mean."

Ada gritted her teeth and stayed silent, but inside felt turmoil. She regretted ever confiding in Knight. She had only done so because they were so lonely, and the nights were long, with nothing to do but talk. He knew little about the intricacies of her marriage or the way her husband beat her, sometimes so badly that she lost children. And, now, he was throwing her vulnerabilities back into her face.

"You aren't good to me," Knight cried out. Her face set in stone, Ada tried to reason with him, but he was clueless about how much work she had done over the past few months to keep them alive: the chopping, sledding, hauling, making the food, and taking care of him. But as soon as she tried to explain, he pummeled her with another slew of insults.

"No wonder your children died. You never took good care of them either," Knight said. Ada listened to him in shock. She had come back to the camp after another hard morning's work to take care of him, and he tore into her where it hurt the most—the loss of her beloved children.

Under his breath, Knight grumbled, "You aren't trying to save me."

She let out a sigh. He knew the end was coming, and he was frightened. They were both starving. Every day her stomach rumbled, tied into knots from the months of eating stringy fox, with no variation in her diet. There were no vegetables or roots or starches. If Knight died, Ada knew she would be left alone on this godforsaken island. He had been lying in bed for nearly nine weeks. Ada didn't want to die alone. She feared no one would find her body and she would just decompose into the wilds.

Ada shook the thoughts from her mind. But she had to be realistic. She needed to prepare for her child's life without her. She wanted Rita, her sister, to raise Bennett. She didn't want his father to lay his hands on their son. She could only imagine the rage with which he would raise their child.

Ada walked over to her bed and pulled out her journal from under her pillow. She wrote every day in its soiled yellow pages and now penned four simple lines: "I wish she take my son. Don't let his father Black Jack take him. If Rita, my sister live. Then I be clear. Ada B. Jack"

Closing the diary, she put it back underneath her pillow. She was so tired, overwhelmed by the sheer powerlessness to change her situation. Ada laid down on her bed, folded her arms around herself, and drifted off to sleep. When she awoke the sun was rising, but she could not will herself to get out of bed to check the traps. Through a sliver of light streaming into the camp, Ada saw a raven between the mountains and the campsite.

Black against the sun, the raven was flying from east to west, a speck in the sky. Ada watched the bird's journey across endless expanses, envying its freedom, until, exhausted, her eyes shut and she drifted off to sleep. The next day was much the same. Weariness enveloped her, coursing through her bones and holding her spirit down. She pulled out the Bible that Knight had given her and read the familiar passages over and over again. She imagined people at that very moment going to church, wearing their finest Sunday clothes, kissing their families, having conversations. Not sitting, like Ada, cold, lonely, and nearly starving, waiting for death to snatch her in its claws.

She had to clear her mind. She was still alive. If she stayed depressed in bed all day, she would wither away and never see her child again. Ada pushed herself up on her elbows, swung her feet over the edge of the bed, and made her way outside. She started to saw wood for the fire, and when hauling it back she was so weak she almost fainted. Ada needed to go back to bed. "I'll just sleep a little bit more," she whispered to herself. But she crawled into her sleeping bag and stayed there. She wasn't feeling well and only woke up occasionally to read the Bible.

The next morning, she woke up to the thump of a book against her head. Knight had used the last of his strength to get Ada's attention. "I'm pretty sick," he hissed. She didn't have the strength to say anything to him. Ada just got out of her sleeping bag, filled his water cup, and went back to bed. She couldn't believe he was still alive. Knight had taken sick so many months ago, and now it was almost May.

As she drifted off to sleep, she began to dream that she was all alone when she saw two men with a dog team come to rescue her. She ran down to them and asked if they were going to find the way out of there. They didn't answer. Nightly her dreams became the place where she was happy and at peace.

In her subconscious she saw her son Bennett—his trusting eyes, almost completely covered by his thick black bangs, and his inquisitive face. They were together, with lots of people. Bennett was looking at a picture of a clear turquoise swimming pool. He kept pointing at the pool and showing it to Ada. She asked her son, "How do you know what a swimming pool is?" When she woke up, Bennett wasn't there, and she realized it was just a dream. He had vanished into thin air.

Ada went back to sleep and around 10 a.m. heard the sound of water dripping. Her head was still foggy, but then she opened her eyes and saw it was Knight's nose. He was raised on one arm on his cot, his nose was dripping bright red blood. He was holding a one-pound tea tin full of blood under his chin. He must have been bleeding for some time. His face was blue, and he suddenly turned his face away from the can and laid still. He looked like he was dead. Ada called out his name sharply. She repeated herself numerous times until finally he whispered that he was okay.

"Do you want some hard bread?" Ada soaked it in oil and fried it, so it felt like the food had some substance.

Knight was just skin and bones in his sleeping bag. Ada had cut a hole in his nightclothes and bag to put a bedpan underneath, and he just lay there, life dripping out of him. Ada had to hold his head so he could sip water. She made a bag from seal sacks, the animals' stomach linings, filled it with cotton, and put it underneath his back because he was so sore. She filled more bags with hot sand and put them under his feet every morning and night.

"If anything happens to me," he whispered. "Put my diary and some papers I've written into my trunk. The key is in my trouser pocket. Look after my camera and rifle, and keep them dry."

By mid-June, the sun was getting stronger and the snow began to melt. The ice floes started to crack and Ada could hear them moan throughout the night. Even though Knight was nearly dead, she still had the will to live. Ada knew she had to prepare in case she needed to survive another winter on Wrangel Island. Now that it was warm, she wanted to use the remaining ammunition to shoot as much game as she could for curing. Ada decided to trek over to the little island where they had first camped upon arriving at Wrangel Island two years earlier.

Ada traipsed over crunchy patches of snow. She was the only human soul on the island. She spotted a seagull nest and peeked in to find three eggs nestled inside. A slow smile spread over her face. She pocketed the eggs to eat them later. First, she wanted to try and catch a seal. They had started to climb out of their long hibernation and sun themselves on the rocks. Suddenly Ada heard the distant sounds of a flock of geese flying overhead. She raised her shotgun, aimed, and pulled the trigger, watching as one of them plummeted to the ground.

Ada stewed the goose until the meat fell off the bone, but by then Knight was too weak to chew. His throat was so sore and Ada knew he wouldn't last much longer. She stood over him, looking down at his drawn face, tears falling down her cheeks, when suddenly Knight's eyes fluttered open. "What is the matter Ada?" he asked. He said it so gently, so differently from the way he had been speaking to her over the past several weeks, that she couldn't help but cry more.

"Try and get along some way until the boat arrives," he said. "It will come." He closed his eyes, and by June 23, Knight was dead. Ada was again alone on the island.

The Sole Survivor

Ada wrote a long letter to the expedition founder, Stefansson, explaining Knight's cause of death, how long he had lingered, and, finally, how he had died. She thought he had passed away peacefully. She didn't think she would survive until the boat arrived, and Ada wanted the others to know what happened to them. Now she was alone again. For some reason that was scarier than being on the island with Knight, although he was abusive and not much help. There was no guarantee the boat would ever arrive. She had no idea if the explorers had arrived at their destination and told the others of their plight. Chances were greater that they died on their journey, succumbing to the frigid cold and desolate landscape.

Ada decided to write a letter to Galle too in the event he made it back. Out of all the explorers on the expedition, she had the most faith in his ability to survive the harsh climate. He would know to look at her typewriter to see if she left any communications. Ada left the letter in the typewriter. If rescuers were able to make it to Wrangel Island, they would come to the camps and find the letters. Ada got up from the desk and packed up her meager things. She couldn't bury Knight's body—the ground was still too hard and her body too frail to make the effort. She took one last look at Knight's still, weathered body and went into another tent they used for storage. She would sleep here now. She didn't want to stay near his corpse.

Three days after Knight died, Ada shot her first seal with his rifle, and a week later, another one. On July 4, she killed her third seal. Ada knew this because she made a calendar out of typewriting paper she cut into small pieces. Each piece marked a specific day. She didn't want to lose track of time. If she did, she would surely lose her mind.

Ada saw another seal, and although she knew she didn't need the meat, she couldn't resist the opportunity. She dropped to her stomach and crawled forward, her finger on the trigger of the rifle, when the seal moved to an ice floe. As she crept toward the water, Ada must have accidentally jostled the gun, and bang!—a bullet slipped out of the barrel into the air, and the seal slipped into the water. Ada smirked. It served her right for getting greedy.

She cleaned herself off and headed back to the camp, which was situated only a few hundred yards from the beach. As she neared the tents, Ada saw another seal. She lifted Knight's rifle and took careful aim. The seal fell and she was filled with relief. At least she wasn't going to lose another one. She needed to obtain and prepare enough salted meat to last through the winter. Summers were short in the Arctic, and it was the perfect time to hunt when the animals were out, fat and lazy.

On the way to get a poling line to drag the seal back to the camp, Ada heard a strange noise, as if thunder was rumbling. Above her the sky was clear blue with a few scattered clouds. She turned around and saw something that looked like a yellow ball of fur hurtling toward her, and she quickly realized it was a polar bear cub. There were 400 yards between her and the tent, and Ada ran as fast as could toward the opening. Before she could catch her breath, she grabbed her field glasses and climbed up to the high platform she used for her bed, which was nestled at the back of the large tent. Narrowing her eye, she could make out the mother bear and her cub tearing apart the seal meat, its bright-red blood staining their snouts.

Ada felt her heart sinking. The polar bears knew where the camp was now. They knew she could catch seals, and they would be back. Predators preferred to scavenge rather than exert the energy and taking on the risks of hunting themselves. She willed herself to be strong and counted the ammunition. She had enough to take a few shots, but she couldn't waste her precious bullets on scaring off the polar bear. She knew one shot wouldn't bring a bear down, and once enraged it would certainly charge. The next morning, Ada went outside and saw the blood marks where the seal had lain.

A few days later the mother bear and cub came back, sniffing around the tents. Ada grabbed the rifle and headed outside. If she got complacent and let them get comfortable, she knew eventually the polar bears would turn and attack her. She didn't want to injure them so they would become enraged and charge, so instead she fired a shot in the air. Bang! The polar bears looked up from their foraging then turned around and ran away. But after a few yards, they stopped and looked back at Ada calmly, as if they were no longer scared. She lifted the rifle up to the sky and fired five more shots until they ran away for good.

Ada trembled with fear. She had scared them away this time, but was using up all of her ammunition.

Outside of her tent was a twenty-five-pound tin of lard, and about three days later, it was gone. There were patterns of tracks around the tent and she could make out the large feet of a mama bear and the smaller feet of a cub. They were watching her. Her defenses were running out.

Ada retreated into the relative safety of her tent. She became wary of going outside, sure she was going to be charged by the bears. Her food supply started to run low and she knew she had to return to the land and start hunting more, as the days were beginning to become colder and shorter. Even though it was August, she could sniff the fall's chill in the air.

Then, while she was preparing dinner inside the tent, she heard a peculiar noise that sounded like a whistle. Maybe it was a duck Ada thought; it wasn't polar bears or seals. She knew their calls by now. She peered out of the tent, but it was foggy and she couldn't see anything through the dense moisture. She decided not to venture outside in case it was a polar bear. Ada picked up the Bible and read for a few hours until she fell asleep. She didn't hear anything else, but the next morning, around 6 a.m., she heard the bleating sound again.

This time she was certain it was a boat horn. Her heart leapt with excitement. She grabbed her field glasses and climbed onto the platform, training her eye outside. On the beach, people were milling around. Behind them, a boat was beached. She almost dropped the glasses but willed herself to stay calm, praying for the boat to come toward her camp. Ada patted down her parka and walked down to the beach to signal the boat.

The captain, a native man, got off the barge, wonder coloring his face that someone was on the desolate island. He looked at Ada and at the camp behind her inquisitively. "Where are the rest of the people?" he asked.

"I am the only one left," Ada said.

Ada Blackjack lived on Wrangel Island for two years. The last few months she was completely alone. Ada Blackjack was the sole survivor of the Stefansson Expedition. She returned to Nome, Alaska, where she raised her son Bennett and lived the rest of her life in anonymity.

Noam Gershony
Road to Gold
Israel, 2006

Two black Israeli Apache helicopters soared through the crisp blue September sky on an attack mission during the 2006 Lebanon War. For thirty-three days Israel had been embroiled in bombing and launching rockets against Hezbollah paramilitary forces. The country was on edge as the sounds of war constantly echoed throughout the landscape.

On that morning, the helicopters flew over the arid, sparse hills of the Negev Mountains in southern Israel. Intent on their targets, the pilots didn't see the daily life that continued to unfold below. Mothers hung wet laundry, children played outside in the dusty sand, and trucks motored along the winding roads, oblivious to the whirling action taking place in the sky above. The people had become accustomed to the sounds of war.

Then, in an instant, the helicopters' rotating tails spun out of control and the giant choppers crashed into each other. Upon impact, the Apaches burst into balls of flames and ejected the two pilots and navigators onboard. The steel machines took nose dives and tumbled rapidly, spinning 6,000 feet until they collided onto the scorched earth below. One of the copilots, Ran Kochbah, died on the spot. The two other combatants were also killed instantly, but Noam Gershony, then just twenty-three years old, survived.

He was ejected from the cockpit and landed on a tan hillside, blood spilling from his injured body. Underneath the hot sun, he completely blacked out, the bodies of his compatriots beside him. The helicopters' blades revolved lazily until they completely stopped. The crackling of the radio calling for the pilots' coordinates kept a staccato beat until the controllers realized something terrible happened. Silence descended over the spoiled war scene.

Within hours, ambulances arrived to transport the shattered but surviving helicopter pilot to get immediate medical care. But when they got there, emergency workers found that they couldn't yet move Noam to the hospital as he was too injured. Almost every bone in his body was broken. Paramedics frantically worked to stabilize his damaged body, while ambulances stood nearby, ready to transport him to the nearest hospital. There were concerns they wouldn't be able to save his life. Emergency workers thought his wounds were too severe.

Gently, they finally secured him onto the stretcher, but on the way to the ambulance, Noam's heart almost stopped and medical workers realized they didn't have enough time to save the pilot this way. His needs were too grave. They needed to airlift the lone survivor of the helicopter crash and his rescuers to the nearest hospital for the best chance to save his life.

A medical helicopter arrived, and Noam was bundled into its fuselage. News had already reached the war-torn nation and citizens were anxiously tracking the developments. In such a small country, Israelis count every soldier as their own brother, son, or friend and were fervently praying for Noam's survival as the medevac slowly lifted into the nighttime sky.

When Noam arrived at Rambam Medical Center, a squat windowed concrete hospital with the most medically advanced equipment and doctors in Israel's largest northern city, Haifa, his life hung on by a tenuous thread. During the flight, his lungs had collapsed, and the medical team had to make an emergency stop at a hospital in Safed to revive him.

Doctors evaluated the extent of his injuries and didn't think he would live through the night. But they never gave up hope or trying.

At 4 a.m., Air Force staff knocked on the Gershony family's door in K'far Saba, a mid-sized city in central Israel. "There has been an air crash, he's been critically wounded," they told Noam's mother, Pnina. A pixie-featured, stout woman with the same curly black hair and determination as her son, Pnina burst into tears upon getting the information, and cried, "What is going on?"

Without releasing any more details, they instructed Noam's parents to come to the hospital right away.

Five days passed before Noam opened his eyes. During that time, he lost a quarter of his entire body weight, and the hospital gown hung on his gaunt frame. A dark growth covered his face and his jaw had been wired shut. His head was closely shaven, all his dark curly hair was gone, and his normally tanned skinned had turned pale and pasty. He could not move or feel his arms or legs. A doctor came to speak with him about his condition.

"You've had an accident," he said, putting it simply.

Noam thought he'd been in a car accident; he had no recollection of piloting the helicopter on that fateful day. A dark cloud hung over his memory. He didn't even remember being in the Negev Mountains. All he wanted to think about was when he could leave the hospital. Although Noam knew he was in bad shape, he still wanted to go home.

The doctor rattled off a laundry list of things wrong with Noam's ravaged body. He had broken vertebrae, a broken shoulder, and fractures in his legs, arms, pelvis, and jaw. One leg moved and the other didn't. Doctors thought he was paralyzed and most likely wouldn't walk again.

Everything had changed for Noam, who had spent the past three-and-a-half years not only as a helicopter pilot, but also as a fan of high-risk sports such as bungee jumping, snowboarding, and riding bicycles. Only 50 out of every 10,000 military recruits are selected for pilot training, and those selected must do a minimum of nine years of military service. His future had seemed secure. After their service, many pilots were welcomed into lucrative high-tech jobs or worked as commercial airline pilots, something it seemed he wouldn't be able to accomplish now. The entire future Noam had envisioned for himself had vanished in an instant. Bleakness lay ahead.

Rehabilitation and Recovery

Six months later, after spending countless hours in bed surrounded by his thirty closest family members and friends, Noam was released from the hospital. He was paralyzed, couldn't walk, but was determined to keep trying. In his time at the hospital, he slowly recovered, gained weight, and his energy had returned. Beit Halochem Center, a 10,000-square-foot rehabilitation center smack in the middle of Tel Aviv, Israel's capital, was the next step of his journey.

A facility dedicated to disabled Army veterans, Beit Halochem was the most comprehensive of five centers of its kind in the country. Injured veterans there could use the multipurpose gymnasium, indoor swimming pool, massage and hydrotherapy unit, and shooting gallery to rehabilitate their disability. The grounds included outdoor playing fields and an Olympic-size swimming pool. It was the perfect place for Noam to concentrate on recovering.

In addition to his rehabilitation, Noam also wanted to regain his life. The previous six months he'd spent in the hospital felt like prison. He hated lying in that bed, getting poked and prodded by doctors, and being woken at dawn by the nurses.

Although he loved his hometown, family, and friends, he didn't want to go back to his parents' house. Noam wanted to gain some semblance of normality. In the hospital, he promised himself he wouldn't get depressed and waste his life feeling sorry for himself. "It's a miracle I survived," Noam told the Israeli media, who closely followed his progress. Now, he wanted to do something about the gift he had been given.

So, along with some friends, he rented an apartment in Tel Aviv that had accommodations for the disabled. At that time, Noam was in a wheelchair full-time. He had yet to stand or take a step, and he needed an apartment that would allow him to access all of the living quarters. It was very rare to get an apartment in the capital that had these types of facilities, and Noam felt fortunate.

Every day he would commute from his apartment to Beit Halochem to work with the onsite physical therapists, doctors, and other staff members. The staff encouraged him to join a sports team, and it was under their guidance that he decided to take up tennis. Noam tried numerous other activities: wheelchair basketball, swimming, and target shooting. But before his accident, Noam had taken five tennis lessons and really enjoyed the sport. He'd never imagined the next time he played the game would be in wheelchair.

Tennis became Noam's main form of rehabilitation. He loved getting out on the court in the sunshine and whacking the ball back and forth across the net. Under the guidance of the coach of Israel's national team, Nimrod Bichler, his agility at holding the racquet while simultaneously moving his wheelchair improved tremendously. As Noam's skills rapidly developed, he started to believe he could compete. He practiced for hours on the courts and became more motivated to succeed. He started to compete at the local level, winning match after match, and his excitement about his ability continued to build.

Beit Halochem sent him to competitions all over the world to see if he could qualify for the Paralympics. In his first international tournament in the Czech Republic, he won first place in the Quad Singles, and his coach knew he was witnessing something special.

By 2011, Noam became the first Israeli player to ever qualify for the tennis master's series in Belgium and won first place.

After participating in the U.S. Open, he got to meet his tennis hero, Roger Federer. In early 2012, he won both the French Open and British Open.

Next up was the 2012 London Paralympics.

Road to Gold

On the day of the 2012 London Paralympics gold-medal match, it was sunny and the skies were blue, without a single cloud, eerily reminiscent of the day Noam crashed six years earlier. Except now, he was in the final wheelchair tennis match of the Paralympics. After easily breezing through his previous matches, Noam was playing the champion match against American David Wagner, the number one–seeded wheelchair tennis player in the world, and a formidable opponent. Noam felt the weight of his goals and Israel's hopes upon his shoulders.

Israel had entered the 2012 Olympics season with high expectations of winning medals, but had yet to grasp victory. On the day of Noam's match, Israel hadn't won any medals in the Olympics or a gold in the Paralympics. Before the match Noam listened to ethnic Jewish music to block out the intense pressure. Although he wasn't religious, the familiar songs were calming as he said a few prayers.

The stands were packed with supporters. There were about 4,000 people in the crowd. He had thirty friends and family members there, wearing white T-shirts with hand-drawn blue Israeli flags on them. His friends from the Israeli Air Force crowded the front rows, clapping and waving national flags. Many of his supporters were so confident Noam would win that they only bought tickets for the final stages of the competition.

Wearing dark wrap-around sunglasses and a white T-shirt with a small white-and-blue Israeli flag, Noam exuded a cool confidence throughout the match as the tennis ball whizzed back and forth on the green court. Wagner was faulting, and Noam was able to bypass his lobs and land his shots expertly out of his opponent's reach. In front of the excited stadium, Noam played increasingly better as the match wore on, and was particularly strong with his returns. He played smart, making accurate shots that produced several wins.

And then it was match point. Noam was playing so well that it took him just twenty-two minutes of tennis to get to that moment. With his right hand, he reached up and threw the ball into the air, the small green sphere spinning, and with his arm smashed the serve into the corner of the court. Wagner never had a chance. The match was over. Noam had won the gold medal.

He wheeled into the middle of the court and pumped his arm, just once.

"We said that no matter what happened on the court, he had already won," said his mother.

With a shy grin on his face, Noam wheeled into the center of the stadium and brought his wheelchair to a stop on the gold medal spot. The crowd cheered and screamed with unbridled passion, thrilled at his victory and journey from war hero to sports hero. Paralympic officials dressed in dark suits approached Noam holding a board with flowers and the gold medal he'd worked so hard to obtain. Noam bent his head, overcome by emotion and everything he had endured over the past few years. The gold medal was slipped around his neck and cheers of "Noam! Noam" rose from the stands as everyone began to chant.

Noam lifted the gold medal in his hand and shook his head in wonder, as if he couldn't believe it had actually happened. He lifted his arms, waving the medal and flowers in victory. The crowd burst into another round of cheers.

During the Israeli national anthem, the Hatikvah, the Israeli flag and two American flags were propped behind the athletes as the swelling music played. Overcome by emotion, Noam burst into tears, cradling his face with his hands as he mouthed the lyrics of the national anthem. The crowd solemnly stood and cried alongside Noam. Supporters threw down Israeli flags to him, immensely proud of their native son. Noam draped a flag over his shoulders.

Noam Gershony continues to train with the Israeli tennis national team and helps instruct other fledgling players. In addition, he volunteers teaching math to underprivileged Israeli children. Noam often visits injured soldiers in hospitals to pass on his experiences. He has carved out a new career as a motivational speaker, traveling around the world to tell people about his story.

Odette Sansom
Mission Gone Wrong
France and Germany, 1942–1945

The message asked the team to go to London. Odette knew right away it was a warning. She felt uneasy about the operation, but there was nothing she could do. Protecting Captain Peter Churchill—or Raoul, as she had been taught to call her immediate superior—at all costs was the mission. That had been the first priority since Odette had arrived via sea to France in November 1942. It was the height of World War II, and Odette Marie Céline Sansom had been recruited into the United Kingdom's Secret Operation Executive, an espionage outfit formed just a few months earlier for a secret mission in France.

There was no reason for Odette to think she would ever be a spy. Born to French parents some twenty-odd years earlier, she'd thought about becoming a nurse, or perhaps a teacher. But it seemed like life had other plans for Odette. The British Navy had called for its citizens to send in pictures of France so they could use the photos to map out where the Germans may be planning attacks. Odette mistakenly sent photographs to the War Office of the coastline of Boulogne, where she had summered so often as a child. That's where she'd met Roy, her English husband, and through her marriage she grew to love her adopted homeland. Eventually she was contacted by the head spy, who found out about her ability to speak both French and English without accents.

She nervously smoothed back her shiny chestnut brown curls, hoping they hadn't sprung too much out of place. She thought of her three daughters and prayed they were all right in the convent school where she had left them. When she became a mother, she never imagined her girls would be without their parents, both of them off fighting in the war. Before she began her life as a spy, she struggled knowing the stress she would place her children under, but in the end decided she needed to support the cause. She couldn't think about the separation from her children now. There were things for which to prepare.

Odette clipped her bangs to the side with a sturdy black barrette purchased in a local French pharmacy. She didn't want to show her curls too much. The barrette made her look like all the other twenty-something French girls left behind in these lakeside towns, pining for their loves fighting in the war and biding their time until they returned. There was a fine balance to be struck.

She pinched her cheeks hard, causing red blotches to accentuate the sharp cheekbones of her face. Her dark eyes glistened, their color brown like velvet, lined by thick lashes and high, arched eyebrows. Odette knew her eyes were her best feature. In the mirror her reflection dazzled back, and Odette was satisfied. There was no reason to always look so dour. She was in France, and Odette knew she had to fit in as a lively French girl, even during wartime circumstances.

Even though she had been working undercover and traveling in dangerous conditions for almost a year, since the head office sent her to France, she knew there was never a moment for complacency. She was playing a role. She knew she had to follow orders, for any mistakes could expose their mission. Although Odette was impulsive, the six months in the field had taught her to be extremely cautious.

Odette had to manage everything on her own, getting the messages back and forth and arranging meetings with sources. But now, Raoul was back, and there was a request to meet a source at Hotel Glaiculles at Talloires. Odette finished primping and waited for Raoul.

The day before, Raoul had sent the others away to a safehouse in the south of France. They were cutting down on the number of assets in the mission working to gather information about German movements in France. They received intelligence and sent it back to the War Office in England. The undercover work was extremely dangerous, and they could be found and killed at any moment if any member of their network folded under the pressure. Raoul felt them being closed in upon, and they needed to travel light.

Just after the clock had struck midnight, a plane had swooped in and picked them up, whisking off the returning agents safely into the velvet night. Odette wished she was on that plane too. She could use a few days' rest on the coast to sit in the sun on the beach and drink a glass of wine, to watch the beautiful people saunter by, where life continued as normal and she could forget about the turmoil of the war and the weight of fear pressing in on her.

After the crew had safely flown away, Raoul wanted Odette and their colleagues to drop off the dynamite and the accompanying containers that the plane had left behind. Although they had the ability to defend themselves if they were suddenly attacked, Odette flinched at the thought of blowing themselves or anyone else up. At the break of dawn, early enough to go unnoticed, they hauled the dynamite down the steps of their hotel and hopped on a boat to cross the lake to Talloires.

Still foggy from the lack of sleep, Odette scanned the breathtaking view, soaking in the fresh mountain air, green hills, and craggy mountains lush against the blue sky. It was a beautiful spring day in April. Crocus heads were slowly starting to unfurl, and buds appeared on trees hugging the shoreline. Quaint yellow, pale pink, and mint-colored houses dotting the shoreline glinted against the sun. Each village was more picturesque than the next. Odette closed her eyes for the duration of the ride, relishing a moment of peace.

Upon crossing the lake, Odette grabbed a waiting bicycle with a straw basket affixed to the front. She cycled along the scenic byway and followed the curving gravel road to the waiting source. She gathered intelligence from her sources and she was glad it all went so smoothly.

Later that evening, as Odette was resting after an exhausting twenty-four hours, as it was always stressful to meet sources and convince them to provide information she needed, Raoul came to her room for a debriefing.

As they spoke, the hotel's elderly owners barged into Odette's room, opening the door in haste without bothering to knock.

In surprise, Odette leapt up, but the intrusion happened in a flash and there was little time to maneuver. Raoul scrambled to hide when he heard the noise. They had been discussing their recent activities and Odette was in the midst of describing her encounter in Talloires. She barricaded the hotel room doorway with her body to shield them from seeing Raoul.

"There are people here to see you," one of the owners said to Odette, standing firmly in the doorway, awaiting an answer. She had no choice but to follow them, discreetly shutting the door behind her as they left.

Raoul knew to stay in the room. The owners didn't see him and no one knew he was there. He was better off staying put and letting Odette handle the situation. If he could be saved, the mission would be considered a success.

Tucked in the center of town, the hotel was small, with just a few rooms. Odette knew they didn't have much time before Raoul was discovered, and there were limited ways for him to escape whoever the visitors were. She had to hold them off. She walked down the damask wall-papered hallway flanked with heavy drapes to find a few Italian men and a tall, thin German man from the Gestapo, their notorious secret police, waiting for her at the end of the hallway.

The German was wearing civilian clothes, a shirt tucked neatly into his slim pants. He had fair hair and large blue eyes. At first, Odette did not realize who he was, but then his face registered in her mind. She had seen him in town before and knew that the Gestapo were there, lying in wait to bring them in at the opportune moment. It was a cat-and-mouse game. There was a short man standing beside the German with his hat pulled down and a dark scarf wrapped around the bottom half of his face, obscuring his features. She felt a shiver of fear pass through her spine but quickly squashed her panic.

The Gestapo reached out his hand, but Odette did not take it.

"I think a lot about you," he said. It was a strange opening line and Odette had to think fast. She needed to keep him distracted in order to give Raoul enough time to escape.

"I don't care what you think," Odette replied, her voice harsh.

But he didn't take the bait.

"You've done a very good job of work, and you almost won the game. It is not your fault that you lost," he said, his voice even and soothing. Odette realized then that this was not going to end well.

She glanced down the hallway and hoped Raoul had made his move.

"I know Raoul is here," the Gestapo said, following her gaze. "Show me how to get to him." Odette hesitated, but then the cold, hard steel of a gun was shoved into her back. The hotel was probably surrounded, she feared Raoul might be shot if he attempted to flee, so she decided to remain calm and take the men to her room.

When Odette opened the door, Raoul spun around and saw the man standing with her.

"They are the Gestapo," Odette said before anyone had the chance to speak.

The men moved forward to arrest Raoul, as they had information that he was a spy, and in the ensuing commotion Odette slyly grabbed his wallet containing messages they had collected earlier that day from their sources. She put the dark leather pouch down the sleeve of her dress, and out of the corner of her eye, saw that Raoul had noticed. He slowly blinked his eyes and Odette understood the messages could never be revealed to their enemies.

The Gestapo brought them outside and loaded Odette and Raoul into a sleek and expensive dark green car. In the driver's seat sat a rakish gentleman wearing a beret. He watched quietly as the doors opened to let in his new passengers, flicking the ashes of his cigarettes out the open window onto the cobblestones below. As they entered the car, Odette deliberately caught the edge of her stocking on the corner of the door. When she bent down to remove the snag, she pulled back a piece of the rough leather and buried the wallet under the back seat of the car, hoping it would never be found. When news of their arrests leaked, she prayed their associates would have enough time to take necessary precautions to either disappear or protect their sources.

On the Way to Annecy

Raoul and Odette were driven to Annecy, the largest town in the region, and put in separate dank barracks. Raoul was placed in a proper cell secured with metal bars, but they put Odette in a closed room with shut windows. The walls were bare and brown. Everything was dark and closed around her. There was no way to get out.

The sound of the door creaking pierced the darkness. Odette opened her eyes into the gloominess of the room. She could barely see a few feet in front of her. It was as if it was endless nighttime. She didn't know how much time had passed when the Italian inspector came into the cell.

"Your husband is a criminal, Madame," he said in French. His voice sounded funny, with a lilting accent.

"Why?" Odette asked, giving him the opening she knew he wanted.

"Well, he tried to escape last night and knocked a man down. The consequences were pretty bad for him," the inspector answered.

Odette nodded her head but did not ask him any more questions. She said nothing. The inspector told her she needed to move into another room, but she knew it was only a ploy to confuse her. The displacement could throw her off. They opened the door to her room and Odette blinked into the light. Only a single day without access to sunlight and she already felt disoriented.

It felt like months had passed since she was sitting in the hotel room with Raoul even though it was just last night. The inspector brought her down a corridor into another room with a blacked-out window. She was sure there were people watching through the reflective pane, but she couldn't see them.

The inspector asked her questions about the work she had been doing, but again she refused to say anything. There was nowhere to sit in the interrogation room and no water to drink. Her strength was beginning to falter and her captors were relentless. They prodded her and got in her face, so close that Odette could smell a hint of wine on the inspector's breath. But still she would not talk.

"You are very strong," the Italian inspector said in admiration. Even though she didn't ask, later on that day the inspector paid her another visit to let her know that Raoul was still alive.

"I am very sorry for you. I know it's very difficult being a woman, and I will try and help you," he whispered. Odette thanked him. She knew how to play the part of the feeble woman. From her time in the field she had learned how to manipulate people and situations to her advantage. As long as she acted grateful and nonthreatening, he would work to protect her. Five or six days passed with the captors coming and going from her room, barraging her with questions. She did not know exactly when she had lost track of time, but around the seventh day the door opened and the inspector came to pull her out.

"Where are we going?" Odette asked, but he didn't answer. Instead he dragged her down a long hallway toward a sliver of the daylight. Happiness rose in her heart. Were they letting her go?

The inspector pulled open the front door, and in a second, Odette was pushed outside. In front of her waited a lorry with wooden seats and slats lining the cargo hold.

They whisked Odette onto the lorry next to Raoul, who was handcuffed to the seats. She jumped in surprise. She was so happy to see him, but dismayed by his condition. They couldn't talk, but she noticed he had a broken finger, bruises on his face, and injuries all over his body. He was in very bad shape. His face was downcast, and it was clear he had suffered more physical abuse than Odette. She felt horribly guilty, as they were both willing to die for the cause, but he had been tortured and she hadn't been. Odette did her best to try and raise his spirits.

Odette Sansom 169

As the truck drove they could start talking freely over the rumble of the tires. There was a mix of Italian and French prisoners being transported alongside them, and no one else spoke English.

As the lorry pulled up in an area Odette recognized as Grenoble, she whispered to Raoul, "We've formed a perfect team. We can trust each other completely, and we would readily lay down our lives for each other." He didn't respond but she could see the gratitude in his eyes as the guards came to take out the prisoners.

They separated Odette and Raoul and put her in a cell with two other women who were apprehended for crossing into the warfront. Through the prison bars she could see Raoul in another cell. She waved to him, but again he was unresponsive. Then, after a week of waiting idly, they were going to be moved to another location: They were headed to Paris.

Isolation, Then Prison

It had been fifteen days, by her count, since she had seen another soul. After she and Raoul had been brought to Paris, Odette was placed in a jail of some sort and had no idea where Raoul had gone. He had just disappeared. There was not a single update. Odette realized she wouldn't be able to expect much kindness from her captors.

At first, they had been polite. The interrogators spoke to her about music and travels. They offered her cigarettes and new blouses. She accepted their gifts gratefully and smoked the cigarettes, one after the other. She changed her blouse, as it was soiled and reeked of sweat. Odette wanted to keep herself clean and attractive. She wanted to look respectable.

And then, the Gestapo officer who had arrested her weeks ago at the hotel in France showed up to interrogate her again. He wasn't wearing a hat or coat, but she knew it was him all the same. He had the same piercing blue eyes and measured way of talking. He spoke beautiful French. Odette could have mistaken him for a Lorrainer, his accent and bearing were so impeccable. He asked her for her real identity and she told him what she had been trained to say, to avoid revealing her true identity at all costs. She knew he didn't believe her, but could tell it didn't matter. There were bigger things he wanted.

"Raoul is Captain Churchill, a nephew of the prime minister?" he asked.

"No!" Odette exclaimed. If the Gestapo thought that was the truth, Raoul would surely suffer. Or maybe they would treat him better if they thought he was so valuable? The Germans may want him to use him as a bargaining chip.

The German was silent for a moment, and then, in a low ominous voice, he said, "I don't believe you, and there are ways of making you speak."

Odette knew then she needed to let the Germans think that Raoul was a relative of Winston Churchill and continue to let them think that she was married to him. The idea just may save them both.

At that point, the door opened, and a Frenchman Odette had never seen before walked in. He was young, in his twenties, with thick dark hair, a sallow complexion, and beautiful, dark eyes fringed with thick, dark lashes. There was something very feminine about him. He was well-dressed, very French in his mannerisms, and spoke with an educated Parisian accent.

But immediately, Odette knew he was evil.

She stiffened and looked around, wide-eyed, but there was no escape.

The two men motioned for her to sit in a narrow, wooden schoolchild's chair located in the center of the room. The tall, thin Gestapo officer walked toward her and grabbed her arms so tightly she could feel the bruises his fingers made as the delicate Frenchman burned her shoulder with fire from a match. She screamed in pain and the stench of flesh filled the air, as if meat was cooking on the fryer. She swallowed to stop herself from vomiting. The pain was excruciating.

Odette shook her head and refused to talk.

The Gestapo officer dropped her arms and her hands fell to her sides. She didn't have the strength to pick them up and check the wound on her shoulder.

"I'll think of something else to make you talk," the German said. He pointed out of the window.

"Look at all of those happy people outside!" he said. Then he turned to her and asked, "Why are you doing this? Is it for money?"

"My father was killed for France," Odette answered tightly. Her father, a soldier for the French army, was killed in World War I. "I'm British, and I love England more than France."

He sighed. "What a pity." Odette felt her stomach curl. Maybe she'd answered wrongly. If he thought she couldn't be bought, what were they going to do to her?

He opened her pocketbook, and the sight of her familiar belongings sent a chill through her body, more so than the burn throbbing on her shoulder. She felt like a different person from the woman who had carried that purse. He rummaged through the contents before asking, "Would you like something from out of here?"

He held out the rosary. Odette's heart swelled at the familiar glass beads. Her mother had given them to her shortly before the war started.

"Would you like this?" he asked. Odette nodded her head. She would love to touch them, just for a moment. They would bring her so much comfort, but just as she leaned forward to take it, he snatched it away and her hand grasped at the air. He asked again about the Churchill connection. Odette didn't answer, but moved her eyes briefly, signaling affirmation. She could tell the Germans believed her and were satisfied. The interrogation stopped.

That afternoon Odette was moved to a prison in Fresnes. She was placed in a cell by herself, without any access to books or other materials. They didn't let her out to exercise, and she wasn't allowed to speak to anyone or have any visitors. She still didn't know what had happened to Raoul. After a few weeks of isolation, Odette felt like she might lose her mind. And then they put her among the other prisoners, common criminals imprisoned for stealing, prostitution, and other sundry crimes. Odette didn't want to have anything to do with any of them, so she kept to herself.

She learned that sources with whom she worked with on previous missions were telling the Gestapo everything they knew and were being treated fairly. Still she decided to stay silent.

Then, one afternoon, the Gestapo brought her a surprise. Raoul appeared in front of her cell. They spoke for about two hours. But it wasn't the same Raoul she remembered—the fearless, rakish leader of their secret mission was no more. He had a furtive look and couldn't maintain eye contact. He was still suffering from his previous injuries, Odette thought, but something wasn't right; he seemed frightened, which wasn't his normal countenance. She chose to keep their conversation light, given the circumstances, and she was on edge that the Gestapo would stop their conversation, but to her surprise they didn't say a word. They chatted about memories of England, and Odette felt her heart contract, wondering if she would ever see her beloved country again.

On a hot July afternoon, she was summoned to Gestapo Headquarters on Avenue Foch in Paris. On the first floor Odette was met by a man who fit the description of Hermann Goering, a senior S.S. officer in Germany's Third Reich. He was a large man, and his chest was decorated with military medals.

"Welcome, Madame Churchill," he greeted her politely. She almost corrected him but decided not to, and she let it go. He pointed the way up the stairs to the top floor, where she was met by another man, who was small and very thin, with a mess of dark hair. Odette believed he was German too.

"Would you like some tea?" he asked Odette. She said no. He pestered her with questions about her sources, but Odette remained coy. After a pause, her interrogator flicked his finger and the door opened. A short man with sandy hair and deep blue eyes limped into the room on one leg. He was well-dressed in pressed flannel trousers, a blue jacket, and a beret fitted on his head. Odette surmised he was about thirty years old.

It took a moment, but Odette recognized the man. His name was Emile, a source she had worked with previously. She swallowed in surprise and willed herself not to blow his cover, although he seemed to be working with the Gestapo. Had she been wrong about him all along? He was smoking a cigarette and grinned at Odette, but she didn't look back at him. Instead, she took a moment to compose her thoughts.

"Do you know him?" her interrogator asked.

"No," Odette answered.

"Yes, we've met before," said Emile. Odette felt rage inside. "I've worked with you and Raoul." She wondered why he was talking like this in front of the Gestapo.

"I'm sorry, I do recognize this man," Odette backtracked. She didn't know what game Emile was playing but she wasn't going down for his mistakes. "I did meet him, but it was at 2 o'clock in the morning for a few minutes."

The interrogator took this as a reasonable answer and didn't bother her again about the discrepancy.

Emile smirked at Odette.

"What about Fresnes? Can you take it?" he said, referring to her current stay in the infamous prison.

"It's all right. I can take it," Odette answered, crossing her arms defiantly.

They went back and forth for several minutes with Emile asking the same question repeatedly and Odette answering the same way. She didn't understand why Emile was there, but tried to hide her confusion by speaking as cordially as she could.

Then, abruptly, Emile got up and left the room. As soon as he was gone, her interrogator asked, "What do you know about that man? Was he working in Cannes with Raoul?"

"I don't know anything about him, really," said Odette. "Raoul never told me anything."

Her interrogator locked eyes with her. Odette broke away first. He was emotionless and she didn't want to trifle with him. She just wanted to get out of the room safely.

"It doesn't matter, you'll both be dead shortly," he said.

Odette didn't respond. She could feel her interrogator's frustration grow.

"You ought to be killed once for France, then once for England," he snapped.

Odette looked up and held her head high. She looked directly at the man's eyes.

"You can only kill a woman once."

Odette was then returned to Fresnes prison, where she spent more than a year. She spent most of her time held in solitary confinement, and she tried to keep herself sane by remembering her time in France when she was free. The faces of her parents often floated through her mind. She was questioned many more times by the Gestapo and had a red-hot poker jabbed in her back and her toenails torn off. She was threatened time and again with worse torture. But she refused to talk.

Right before she heard she was being transferred to Germany, Odette saw Emile one last time at Avenue Foch. He didn't look well and he was much thinner. She understood his predicament.

By this time, she too suffered greatly from chronic stomach and glandular pain.

He entered the room where Odette was waiting with seven other women who were also being sent to Germany.

"How are you?" Emile asked, the familiar grin playing on his face.

"Did you know your brother has gone to Germany?" she said. A close cellmate had passed her the information. Emile did not respond and moved on to talk to another woman in the group.

Before Odette had a chance to say anything else, a truck arrived and the women were handcuffed and taken on board. It was November 1944.

She never saw Emile again.

Ravensbrück Concentration Camp, Germany

Throughout the trip to Germany, they stopped at many different locations, each one successively worse than the last. Odette was placed in cells with other women, sometimes fifty of them packed into one location. There were no sanitary facilities or places to go outside. It was suffocating. They were barely served food, and water was scarce.

One night while in Frankfurt, Odette had to sleep on the floor with thirty other women, gritty pieces of sand flying into her nose and eyes. The conditions were unbearable, and she shut her eyes in an effort to escape the misery of the experience. Many of the other prisoners had dysentery. Odette was constantly questioned by the Gestapo, who struck her on the face repeatedly. After this inquietude, they told Odette they were moving her to Ravensbrück, the infamous northern German concentration camp exclusively for women, located approximately 90 kilometers from Berlin.

Ravensbrück was located on a field of barren soil with nary a tree in sight—just long rows of squat brick barracks punctuated by glass windows every few feet. Situated at each end of the camp were brick ovens, acrid smoke piping out of each chimney and filling the heavy gray air. Ten-foot flames shot out of the brick contraptions, and there was an overbearing smell. When Odette arrived, she surveyed the terrain apprehensively as she had heard about concentration camps, horrible stories about torture chambers where they slaughtered Jews and enemies of the Reich. But Odette had never seen evidence of one, until now. Involuntarily, she shivered, then collected herself. On the way here, the Gestapo guard had told Odette she was destined for death along with the eight other women accompanying her.

He had looked over the convoy of scared women. "None of you will come back alive," he'd said. "And you will be made to suffer before they get rid of all of you."

Some of the women cried out in response to his warning, but Odette didn't show her emotions. She'd learned that the Gestapo and Nazis capitalized on moments of weakness and would exploit any opening.

The first night at the camp, Odette was forced to sleep on the floor of the showers without a blanket, shivering in the frigid air. There was no food, and Odette could feel hunger pangs gnawing at her stomach. She didn't see anyone until the next morning, when a Gestapo officer took her to the camp commandant, Suhren, who had been informed that Odette was Raoul's wife and was a Churchill. She deflected his interest by murmuring that

Raoul was a distant relation of the prime minister, but was careful not to say too much.

"Then you better use another name," Commandant Suhren advised her abruptly. "Don't let the other inmates know there is an important person in this camp." He barked an order in German, and another Gestapo came in to lead Odette out of his office. She was taken to cell number 42, in the basement. The room measured ten feet long, five feet wide, and eight feet high. There was a small window covered with bars, frosted glass, and a radiator grill, giving practically no light or ventilation. The furniture consisted of a table, a wooden bunk with a sleeping bag, two blankets, and a stool. She was all alone in the cell.

The radiator was heated on full pressure and Odette's tiny cell was burning hot. She could not touch the radiator, and there was no way to turn it off or regulate the heat. During the day, she was forced to sit in the cell wearing just a slip, and at night, she ran her blankets under cold water in order to get some sleep. Her glands swelled from the excessive heat, and she could breathe only with great difficulty.

In the morning, guards would bring in a cup of coffee and a small slice of bread, which would be all the nourishment she would receive that day. Occasionally, her jailer would bring a bowl of soup and, sometimes, a slice of cheese on the bread or a potato. Odette never forgot the kindness. One month later the food stopped coming, and she went a week without eating. Odette asked for food, but none ever came. She became too weak to sit up and was about to give up, when the warden finally came to her cell with food and explained, "We got you mixed up with another prisoner. We weren't supposed to take food away from you."

By the time the food arrived, Odette was too sick to eat. The S.S. guards took her to see the doctor, who told her that her swollen glands and temperature were a result of tuberculosis. When they sent her for x-rays, she was petrified. She knew if the Nazis knew she had a disease, they would surely kill her. Her hair started to come out in clumps each night.

When the guards came to get her one day, Odette was sure this was the end. Instead they took her to get ultraviolet treatment for her condition. She went twice a week to the doctor and was moved out of her cell into a bunker on the ground floor.

Her conditions were far better than they had been in the basement cell. She could see daylight and breathe in fresh air. She was in a block of thirty-eight cells all of the same size. Each cell held ten to twelve women, mostly Russians, Poles, and a few Germans. All day long Odette could hear a mishmash of languages she couldn't begin to understand. At night, though, she could hear the sounds of women being beaten elsewhere in the building. Odette could hear their screams and their abusers counting in German as they whipped the prisoners. She would close her eyes and count thumps of the beatings in her mind. They were given only one meal a week, and most of the women had deteriorated to skin and bones.

France seemed so far away. Even farther was England. In between the beatings, executions took place in front of the crematorium, and she could hear the shots being fired. Odette could barely sleep at night. She had no news of Raoul. She didn't know if the home office knew where she was being kept or if they even knew she was still alive. Odette desperately wanted to open the window in the bunker but knew if she did that a layer of ash would float into the room from the crematorium that had been running day and night since January.

There was no longer any attempt to mask the fires during air raids. They just let them run non-stop. It was already April, more than a year since she had been arrested on that fateful day in France, and it seemed that Odette had little chance of ever being free again.

On the morning of April 27, 1945, Commandant Suhren came to Odette's cell. She hadn't seen the commander in weeks as the air raids had become more frequent, the planes screaming overhead at all hours. The camp was emptying of people at a dizzying pace. Every day, Odette heard the doors to neighboring bunkers open and hordes of women being escorted out to their deaths. So, when Suhren came to her cell door, Odette was sure her time had come. He made a cutting gesture across his throat and motioned for her to gather her things.

Odette packed up her meager belongings, and around 8 a.m., an S.S. officer arrived and led her outside along with a German girl. Suhren suddenly appeared again and put the two of them inside a prison van loaded with medical supplies and about six other people, some of whom Odette recognized from her weeks at Ravensbrück. One was a commander in the Italian navy, the other a Pole who was a well-known racehorse owner. They drove out of the camp and around 10 p.m. arrived at a smaller camp. They stayed there for three days without any water or beds until the afternoon of May 2. Odette was told the commandant wanted to see her and she went outside to see Suhren standing with two Polish girls. He motioned for the three of them to get into a waiting car and there was nothing Odette could do but oblige.

Although Odette didn't know it, Suhren's plan was to surrender himself to the Americans so he could survive. His idea was to exchange Odette, whom he still thought was somehow related to Winston Churchill, to the Americans. In return he hoped the allies wouldn't kill him.

The women settled into the back seat when the commandant turned around, "I'm taking you to the Americans," he said gruffly, and they sped off. They were surround by S.S. convoys as they drove for what seemed like hours. They finally arrived in a small village, where a contingent of American soldiers was waiting. Commandant Suhren stopped the car, and without hesitation, Odette pushed open the passenger door and stumbled toward the waiting Americans.

She was free at last.

Odette Marie Céline Sansom was held captive by the Germans for 375 days, with almost all of her time spent in solitary confinement. American soldiers returned her to England, where she was awarded the George Cross medal—the only living woman to receive the award—for her bravery during World War II. In 1947, after divorcing her first husband, Odette married Raoul, whose real name was Peter Churchill. Their marriage lasted until 1956. During the Hamburg Ravensbrück trials, she testified against S.S. officers and sent Commandant Suhren to his death. He was hanged for his war crimes. Odette died in 1995. She was 82 years old.

References

Juliane Koepcke, page 11

"Air Crashes Links Two Lives Half a World Apart." *Arizona Republic,* January 29, 1972.

Gamarra, Ciro. "Teenage Girl Walks to Safety from Christmas Eve Plane Crash." *Princeton Daily Clarion,* January 5, 1972.

"Girl Survives Airliner Crash, Jungle Trek." *The Times Herald,* January 5, 1972.

"Girl Survivor, in Jungle 10 Days, Helps Locate Plane Wreck." *The Boston Globe,* January 5, 1972.

Koepcke, Juliane. "The Woman Who Fell from the Sky and Lived," Interview by Matthew Banister, Outlook, BBC World Service, March 20, 2012. Audio, 0:28. https://www.bbc.co.uk/programmes/p00pkc3y.

McDonald, Katherine. "Survival Stories: The Girl Who Fell from the Sky." *Readers Digest.* Accessed December 10, 2018. https://www.rd.com/true-stories/survival/survival-stories-the-girl-who-fell-from-the-sky.

"Plane Survivor Tells About Jungle Ordeal." *Arizona Republic,* January 6, 1972.

"Plane Victims Kin Hopeful," *The Sentinel,* January 6, 1972.

"Saga of Juliane Koepcke." *Colorado Springs Gazette Telegraph,* January 8,1972.

"Saga of Juliane Koepcke." *The Columbus Telegram,* January 11, 1972.

"Teen Girl Gets out of Jungle." *The News-Palladium,* January 5, 1972.

"Teens Long Jungle Trek Ends Happily." *The News Palladium,* January 5, 1972.

Henri Nemy, page 29

"Another Miner Saved." *New York Tribune,* April 5, 1906.

"The Courrieres Disaster." *Marlborough Express,* April 25, 1906. https://paperspast.natlib.govt.nz/newspapers/MEX19060425.2.2.

"The Courrieres Disaster Rescue of Another Entombed Miner." *The Times of London,* April 5, 1906.

"The Courrieres Mine Disaster." *The Times of London,* May 4, 1906.

"Lived for Days on Putrid Horsemeat," *The Oakdale Graphic,* April 4, 1906.

"Many Miners Perish in French Colliery." *The San Francisco Call,* March 11, 1906.

"Many Left Dead in Mines," *The Sun,* March 13, 1906.

Mining Institute. "Report on the Mining Disaster on March 10, 1906, at Courriéres, pas de Calais, France." Accessed November 30, 2018.

Neville, Robert G., "The Courrieres Colliery Disaster, 1906." *Journal of Contemporary History* vol. 13, no. 1 (January 1978): pp. 33–52. Accessed November 30, 2018. https://doi.org/10.1177/ 002200947801300103.

"Outlets Cut Off by Fire." *The San Francisco Call,* March 11, 1906.

"Rescued from Living Death." *New York Herald,* March 31, 1906.

"Safe in a Living Tomb," *The Baltimore Sun,* March 31, 1906.

Special dispatch. "1193 Miners Perish in Explosion in a French Colliery." *The Call*, March 11, 1906. https://www.newspapers.com/image/80912106.

"Taken from Mine After Twenty Days." *The San Francisco Call*, March 31, 1906.

Enietra Washington, page 47

Ceasar, Stephen. "Doctor Tells of Effort to Save Victim." *The Los Angeles Times*, March 2, 2016.

Ceasar, Stephen. "Grim Sleeper Victim Recalls 1989 Attack." *The Los Angeles Times*. February 26, 2016.

Ceasar, Stephen. "Grim Sleeper Victim Testifies." *The Los Angeles Times*. February 26, 2016.

Ceasar, Stephen. "Jury Hears Closing Arguments." *The Los Angeles Times*, May 3, 2016.

Ceasar, Stephen. "Sketch Artist Testifies in 'Sleeper' Trial." *The Los Angeles Times*, March 23, 2016.

Gerber, Marisa. "Defense Tries to Cast Doubt in Sleeper Case." *The Los Angeles Times*, May 3, 2015.

Gerber, Marisa. "Grim Sleeper Killer Is Sentenced." *The Los Angeles Times*, August 11, 2016.

Melley, Brian. "L.A. Man Guilty in 'Grim Sleeper' Serial Killings." *Associated Press*, May 6, 2016.

Melley, Brian. "Prosecutor: Evidence Speaks for the 10 'Grim Sleeper' Victims." *Associated Press* May 3, 2016.

Nazaryan, Alexander. "An Elegy For His Victims." *The Los Angeles Times*, July 9, 2017.

Redstall, Victoria. "Grim Sleeper Trial—Enietra Washington Speaks." YouTube, August 11, 2016. https://www.youtube.com/watch?v=s5YUzxKcn-s.

"Sleeper." *The Desert Sun*, May 6, 2016.

Mauro Prosperi, page 63

20th Century Fox. "Shouldn't Be Alive—Mauro Prosperi." 2016. December 23, 2015. https://www.youtube.com/watch?v=cPEBrDThuVY.

Gander, Kashmira. "Marathon Runner Mauro Prosperi Drank Urine and Ate Bats, Snakes, and Lizards to Survive in the Desert for Over a Week." *The Independent,* November 27, 2014. https://www.independent.co.uk/news/world/europe/marathon-runner-mauro-prosperi-drank-urine-and-ate-bats-snakes-and-lizards-to-survive-in-the-desert-9888424.html.

Prosperi, Mauro. "Lost in the Desert: The Extraordinary Survival of Mauro Prosperi," Interview by Matthew Banister, *Outlook*, BBC World Service, November 27, 2014. Audio, 0:12. https://www.bbc.co.uk/programmes/p02cww26.

Ridley, Sarah. "Man Lost in Sahara Desert for Ten Days Drank Urine and Bat Blood to Survive." *The Mirror,* November 27, 2014. https://www.mirror.co.uk/news/uk-news/man-lost-sahara-desert-ten-4705299.

Coach Ek and the Wild Boars Soccer Team, page 79

Cheung, Helier and Tessa Wong. "The Full Story of Thailand's Extraordinary Cave Rescue." BBC News, July 14, 2018. https://www.bbc.com/news/world-asia-44791998.

Fedschun, Travis. "Thai Cave Boys Were Actually Handcuffed, Heavily Sedated, during Dramatic Rescue." Fox News, January 15, 2019. https://www.foxnews.com/world/thai-cave-boys-were-actually-handcuffed-heavily-sedated-during-dramatic-rescue-new-book-suggests.

Flynn, Sean. "The Thai Cave Rescue: Miracle at Tham Luang." *GQ,* December 3, 2018. https://www.gq.com/story/thai-cave-rescue-miracle-at-tham-luang.

Gormley, Shannon. "Into the Dark." *MacClean's*, January 25, 2019. https://www.macleans.ca/thai-cave-rescue-heroes.

Hutchison, Bill and James Longman. "Boys Rescued from Thai Cave 'Overwhelmed' When Divers First Arrived." *ABC News*, August 23, 2018. 2019, https://abcnews.go.com/International/young-soccer-players-rescued-thai-cave-world-teaching/story?id=57331218.

Nace, Trevor. "The Science Behind Thailand's Unstable Caves." *Forbes*, July 9, 2018. https://www.forbes.com/sites/trevornace/2018/07/09/thailand-cave-rescue-the-science-behind-thailands-unstable-caves/#62d0b6b07095.

Wright, Rebecca and Angie Puranasamriddhi. "Boys, Soccer Coach Trapped in Thai Cave Exchange Notes with Families." CNN, July 12, 2019. https://edition.cnn.com/2018/07/07/asia/thai-cave-boys-notes-intl/index.html.

Wright, Stephen. "Everyone Is Strong in Mind and Heart." *The Gazette*, January 12, 2018.

Josiah Mitchell, page 95

Burdette, J. G. "4,300 Miles: The Clipper Hornet and Her Survivors." *Map of Time*, September 27,2012. https://jgburdette.wordpress.com/2012/09/27/4300-miles-the-clipper-hornet-and-her-survivors.

"Burning of the American Ship Hornet." *The Pacific Commercial Advertiser*, June 30,1866.

Krause, Kristin. *Last Voyage of the Hornet*. Unionville, NY: Royal Fireworks Publishing Co., 2016.

Mitchell, Josiah A. *The Diary of Captain Josiah A. Mitchell 1866*. Hartford, CT: Lockwood and Brainard Company, 1927.

"The New York Clipper Ship Hornet Burned at Sea." *New York Herald*, July 17, 1866.

"The Rescued from the Hornet." *The Montana Post*, August 4,1866.

Steutermann Rogers, Kim, "The Harrowing Journey of the Hornet that Gave Mark Twain His Big Newspaper Scoop." *Honolulu Magazine*, July 26, 2016. http://www.honolulumagazine.com/Honolulu-Magazine/July-2016/The-Harrowing-Journey-of-the-Hornet.

Twain, Mark. "Awful Sufferings at Sea." *New York Herald*, August 27, 1866.

Dina Mironovna Pronicheva, page 115

Berhoff, Karel C. "Dina Pronicheva's Story of Surviving the Babi Yar Massacre." In *The Shoah in Ukraine,* ed. Ray Brandon and Wendy Lower. Bloomington, Indiana: Indiana University Press, 2008.

European Holocaust Research Infrastructure Course in Holocaust Studies. "Babi Yar Survivor Dina Pronicheva Describes Her Ordeal to Soviet Historians, 24 April 1946." Accessed November 1, 2018, https://training.ehri-project.eu/b09-babi-yar-survivor-dina-pronicheva-describes-her-ordeal-soviet-historians-24-april-1946.

United States Holocaust Memorial Museum, RG-23.34.04, "Dina Pronicheva, a Jewish Survivor of the Babi Yar Massacre, Testifies at the War Crimes Trial in Kiev, Ukraine."

Yad Vashem. "The Untold Stories of the Jews in the Occupied Territories of the Former USSR—Testimony of Pronicheva about the Annihilation of the Jews in Babi." Accessed November 15, 2018. https://www.yadvashem.org/untoldstories/database/writtenTestimonies.asp?cid=902&site_id=1260.

Ada Blackjack, page 133

Blackjack, Ada. *Ada Blackjack Papers, 1923–1983, Folder 5: Story of Stefansson Expedition.* Hanover, NH: Dartmouth College, undated.

Blackjack, Ada. *Ada Blackjack Papers, 1923–1983, Folder 3: Typescript of Ada Blackjack Diary.* Hanover, NH: Dartmouth College, undated.

Noam Gershony, page 151

Aharoni, Oren. "Israel Wheelchair Tennis Team Clinches Silver in World Team Cup." *YNetnews.com*, May 7, 2017.

Alster, Paul. "The Reluctant Hero." *The Jerusalem Report*, November 17, 2014.

The FIDV. "The Sky Is the Limit—The Story of Noam Gershony." You Tube, June 23, 2017. https://www.youtube.com/watch?v=R3yePs6lnYl.

Levy, Sue Ann. "Hero Overcame Near-Death Injuries to Win Paralympic Gold." *Toronto Sun*, February 25. 2018.

Silverstein, Barbara. "Injured IDF Vet Turns Lemons into Lemonade at Paralympics." *The Canadian Jewish News*, February 8, 2018.

Odette Sansom, page 161

"G. C. Heroine and Horror Camp," *The Northern Daily Mail*, December 16, 1946.

Imperial War Museums of the UK. "Odette Sansom GC," https://www.iwm.org.uk/history/odette-sansom-gc.

The National Archives of the UK. "Personnel Records Odette Marie Celine HALLOWES, nee BRAILLY, aka Odette SANSOM, aka Odette CHURCHILL."

The National Archives of the UK. Witness Deposition: Odette Marie Celine SANSOM: In The Matter of War Crimes of the Ill Treated Allied Personnel and Atrocities Committed at Ravensbruck Concentration Camp.

About the Author

Cara Tabachnick reports on crime, justice, and conflict in the U.S. and abroad. Her work touches on all aspects of policing, prisons, drugs, technology, and violence.

She has written for publications such as *Marie Claire*, *"O" Oprah Magazine*, *Bloomberg Businessweek*, *The Washington Post Magazine*, *The Wall Street Journal*, *The Christian Science Monitor*, *The Guardian*, and *Scientific American*.

From 2008 to 2015, Cara was the deputy director of the Center on Media, Crime, and Justice at John Jay College of Criminal Justice in New York City. While there, she also served as the managing editor of the daily news service The Crime Report.

She is a graduate of Columbia University School of Journalism and divides her time between Brooklyn, New York, and southern Spain.

Made in the USA
Las Vegas, NV
04 December 2023